LIVING IN THE HEART OF THE UNIVERSE

EXPANDING YOUR RELATIONSHIP WITH EARTH AND THE COSMOS

MEG BEELER

Living in the Heart of the Universe

Expanding Your Relationship with Earth and the Cosmos

Book layout and typesetting: Vladimir Zavgorodny
Cover design: Pete Garceau

Library of Congress Cataloguing-in-Publication Data
Beeler, Meg.
    Living in the Heart of the Universe: Expanding Your Relationship with Earth and the Cosmos / Meg Beeler
        p.   cm.
Includes endnotes and index.
ISBN 978-0-9972765-1-0 (pbk.)
1. Shamanism 2. Andean cosmovision 3. Earth—spiritual aspects 4. Self-actualization (Ecopsychology) 5. Consciousness—spiritual aspects. I. Beeler, Meg II. Title

Published by Earth Caretakers Press
16100 Sobre Vista Court
Sonoma, CA, 95476

Printed in the United States.
First Edition

CONTENTS

LIST OF PRACTICES

PREFACE
MY ENCOUNTERS
WITH THE UNIVERSE

I began trying to understand the universe when I was five years old. "God is omnipotent, omnipresent, and infinite," said my mother.

I tried to imagine God being everywhere and in everything. I tried to imagine going on forever—what did infinity look like? My young self kept thinking about infinity while I climbed trees, caught polliwogs in the creek, and hiked in the hills with the older kids.

I am still curious. You could say that I have spent my life seeking portals into these mysteries.

Some portals I discovered primarily in spiritual realms: meditation, shamanic journeying, and qi gong. Some portals were predominantly physical for me: backpacking, growing my food organically, and working as a potter with clay from the earth. And some portals I found in the wisdom of indigenous cultures.

Forty years into my musings about the universe, I was taught an ancient way of healing. By connecting your own heart energy with the energy of earth and cosmos, you experience yourself as an integral part of the energetic flow between all living things.

A few days after my first experience of this healing, I found myself traveling to the stars. From a bench under a vast sky in the Southern hemisphere, my astral body floated up into blue-black space; my heart expanded into the cosmos. I began to experience the infinity I had imagined for so long.

In that moment, I knew this world of stars and universes would be endlessly interesting: my life's trajectory changed. Thus began my ongoing journey with the Q'ero nation and other Quechua-speaking people of the Andes. I vowed I would return again and again to learn from this culture in which talking to the stars is a normal part of life.

As I learned more about the breathing, conscious universe, my excitement grew. I discovered that like us, the universe is made of the elements in stardust. Like us, the universe is alive, aware, and interconnected with all its parts—from you and me to the multiverses beyond.[1] And I knew that feeling our way into these interconnections feeds our opportunity and potential for "dreaming a new dream" for the planet.

Yet I discovered that my own loneliness, isolation, despair, and sense of being stuck were holding me back. I could not dream a new dream when I was relying on the same assumptions, thought patterns, habits, and stories that had defined my life. None of us can. This is why I have written *Living in the Heart of the Universe*, to share the paradigm-shifting ways of seeing that have been transformational for me and so many of my students.

The heart of the universe, I have learned, is energy, light, vibration, and power. To connect with the cosmic heart is to experience all of creation through your human heart, to put yourself in dialogue and communication with the earth and the cosmos.

For decades now I have visited, learned to perceive, and listened to energy. I have explored our human connections with the living earth and cosmos, weaving ancient indigenous wisdom with my own experience, training, teaching, and healing.

Most of my learning has been experiential. When you work with indigenous people who simply live—who do not put many words around what they experience in their hearts and their bones—you do the same. If you want meaning and mental understanding, you largely have to figure it out for yourself.

In bringing forth the beautiful indigenous wisdom I have experienced, I deeply honor those who have shared their worldview with me. I have tried to stay true to the heart of that wisdom, while also translating the perceptions and practices I have learned into a flow that will be meaningful for you.

Learning to focus my attention and move my energy, release what does not serve me, and fill, instead, with the living energies of the earth and the cosmos changed my life. I hope that learning these tools will change yours too. In guiding you into experiencing your own connection with the living universe, my intent is to help you shift your perception, vision, energy, and story. In this way, we can dream a different world together.

INTRODUCTION
LIVING ENERGY, CONNECTION, AND PERCEPTION: HOW THIS BOOK WEAVES THE THREADS

We live in a world of energy. An important task at this time is to learn to sense or see the energy of everyone and everything: people, plants, animals. This becomes increasingly important as we [move into] the World of the Fifth Sun, for it is associated with the element ether—the realm where energy lives and weaves.

—*Carlos Barrios* [1]

Imagine yourself, as you read this book, surrounded by a spiral of thin gold filaments. Each filament is a thread you can follow, unravel, and reweave into your own energy field. Now imagine the gold filaments spreading out in all directions. Which one will you follow? Which ones call to you?

Imagine a cosmos where all living beings are connected—through heart, energy, breath, and consciousness. Imagine a society where we humans and other creatures live in resonance, attuned to each other's deepest selves. Imagine living your deepest potential in this resonant, vibrant world, forming connections of trust, heart, and reciprocity in all your endeavors.

Imagine living in such a world—right now.

This book will guide you in exploring simple, practical ways you can connect with the energy, mystery, and power of nature, stars, and the universe. This is what I call Energy Alchemy—practices, insight, and inspiration to guide you into transformative experience, aware-ness, and heart opening.[2] Energy Alchemy is based on an ancient and life-changing premise: that you can work with and change your ener-gy—not just your mind and emotions—to shift your experience of and engagement with the world.

You will learn to shift from the heaviness in your life into the beauty of connection. You will discover your harmony and balance returning, your self-doubt and isolation morphing into vitality and joy, and your essence shining as you develop your energetic connection with all that is.

In the process, you will learn to experience all parts of the living universe as alive and responsive to you. You'll learn how to exchange energy with wind and sun, trees and mountains. You will experience yourself as part of the whole, not separate.

Reinvigorating your direct energetic experience is a heart-opening path of beauty that will enable you to find your way back into relation-ship with all beings. Expanding your personal energy to incorporate nature, earth, and cosmic energies will help you draw power from beyond the personal. It will change your life, your stories, and the ways you perceive and engage with the world.

Not so long ago, your ancestors lived in conscious relationship with the living energy of all things. Your cells remember this; your heart remembers this.

Shifting your perceptual awareness to re-enchant your connection with nature is not as difficult as you might imagine. Nor is it difficult to experience, see, and access the living energy we all share. It is wholly within your power to create and establish new patterns of relationship and possibility. It is wholly within your power to move your life and your world into a resonant, sustainable future. This book is your invi-tation to do exactly that.

FOLLOWING THE THREADS

When you are embarking on a new path it is helpful to know where you are going, and how.

This introduction will acquaint you with the key concepts and principles that are woven into the book. Some may be deeply familiar to you. Others may seem contradictory to culturally dominant ways of thinking. Still other principles are tied deeply to indigenous ways of living, or are woven together in ways that may be unfamiliar to you. All of them—concepts, principles, and ways of perceiving—you'll meet repeatedly as you explore your own experiential connections with the heart of the universe.

You'll find a brief anatomy of the book—how the book is organized and ways you can explore it—at the end of this introduction.

WHAT IS LIVING ENERGY?

Everything is made of energy, of waves and patterns of light and vibration. This is true everywhere: in your body, in a river, in the cosmos.

When you want to change anything—inside or out—you have to learn how to work with energy. It is that simple.

All of us exchange energy with everything else, constantly. Energy animates and permeates all of creation, from vibrating electrons to expanding dark matter. Energy's natural state is constant movement (change); when movement stops, energy stagnates.

You can think of your energy as pure potential: it may create, it may destroy, or it may form into something else. There is no judgment in the world of energy: it is not good or bad; it just moves. Everything arises and passes away in continual rhythms.

This web of energy that connects us is holographic, and nonlocal: every part of the web is connected to every other part, and each piece mirrors the whole web. In this universal field, every living being is equally important in the web of partnership and interdependence that supports you and all living beings.

These premises are central to what you will learn about energetic transformation.

IS EVERYTHING REALLY ALIVE?

Historical streams of thought have cumulative, river-like effects on our behavior and thinking. The way we frame reality, and the concepts we take for granted, can limit us.

You may be challenged, like most of us raised in the Western world, to trust your experiences with energy, spirit, and heart. You may have to work to feel connected rather than isolated. You may have assumptions that get in the way of engaging with the living energy in everything around you.

For example, you may have been taught to view yourself at the top of a hierarchy: "lesser" beings such as animals, rocks, and insects are presumed to have little or no consciousness, soul, or feelings. These other beings, you assume, are here to serve you. Your thinking and your behavior are dominated by disconnection from nature.

You may have learned to treat everything as separate. Tree, water source, and butterfly are distinct from you, the person. Food and toilet paper come from a store. Water comes from a bottle. In this separation and fragmentation you may have lost some of your compassion for others.

You may look to technology rather than relationship to solve problems. In fact, you probably believe technology will help humanity understand all of life.

Western views have become *conceptual* rather than *perceptual*, influenced by ideas rather than direct experience. About four hundred years ago when science and religion took divergent paths, spirit became the domain of religion, while the physical world was given over to science. Newtonian, atomistic, reductionist views of everything came to dominate our thinking. Conceptually, this means you've probably learned to depend only on material, tangible, physical measurements to understand the world: if you can't measure and see something (like energy), it doesn't exist. Such duality deeply affects your perspective. And you can choose to perceive differently. As Tibetan Bon master Tenzin Wangyal Rinpoche writes, "How we see the world determines the quality of our practices and our lives."[3]

THE INDIGENOUS VIEW
OF LIVING ENERGY

Indigenous wisdom keepers have perceived and used energy to change the trajectory of their lives for a very long time. In fact, most of your ancestors, if you trace back far enough, related to the living energy in all things as a natural part of their lives. You can find evidence of this in story, myth, ancient cave paintings, stone carvings, and living indigenous ceremony in cultures around the globe.

Despite globalization and the destruction of indigenous life ways, many wisdom cultures have retained practice and prophesy regarding cosmic energy changes that continue to inform us. By fostering their relationship with and understanding of the movements of the stars, they prophesied the galactic shift into a new fifty-six-thousand-year cycle that occurred in 2012—the "turning over of the world."[4] The Q'ero of Peru—whom I was blessed to meet many years ago—intentionally came out of their isolated, high mountain homes to share their worldview and their version of this prophesy with people around the globe.[5]

The vision and practices of the Andean people offer an incredible resource to people like you and me who want to reconnect with nature, earth, stars, and universes. Because they preserved a sense of the whole—and holy—and have intentionally brought their vision to the North, we can learn directly from their ways of seeing everything as alive.

The Q'ero engage with the cosmos of living energy—*kawsay*—in all aspects of daily life, ceremony, story, community, language, weaving, and farming. They move energy—releasing the heavy and filling with lighter, more refined energy—as you will learn to do. They practice reciprocity and seek to maintain alignment and balance. I have woven their ways of being and perceiving into this book.

Living in the Heart of the Universe is rooted in this Andean tradition. The nature-based practices you will learn—experiential translations from their culture to ours—will lead you into reconnection, your potential, and your own lightness of being.

Many cultures besides the Q'ero perceive and engage with the living energy in all things. Chinese wisdom keepers call it *qi*; yogis work with *prana*; and there are nearly a hundred words in as many languages for living energy. All these words describe the animating life force in everything from the smallest subatomic particle to the largest galaxy.

When you learn to experience the aliveness in everything, your sense of connection to, alignment with, and perception of the whole world shifts.

ENERGY AT THE HEART OF THE UNIVERSE

Long before humans had telescopes with which to view the stars and planets, the living energy universe was perceived as the original, subtle womb energy of the cosmos; called the *Akashic field* in ancient texts, it was the source of everything.[6] Mystics, visionaries, and philosophers of all spiritual persuasions have sought this universal essence throughout human history.

The heart of this living energy universe is a cosmic field, implicate, enfolding, and infinite.[7] It contains within it creation and destruction, what has been and what may be. It is a place of excitement and rest, creativity and release, brilliance and mystery. It has been called a consciousness, both inclusive and limitless.

What's incredible to understand is that the heart of our universe is alive, vibrating energy. It is a sea of potential—a void, empty but full of all possibility—communicating with us and within us across space and time. This vital energy pervades all forms, both animate and inanimate. You can draw on this potential! Your intimate and intricate interconnections within this field will help you expand your relationship with the living energy universe.

Seeing living energy as a *model* of the universe gives you a profound and transformative way to perceive and make sense of reality. By weaving ancient wisdom and quantum perceptions together, and exploring your direct relationship to the living energy in all things, you can feed your interconnections, your sense of belonging, and your ability to survive and thrive.

The possibilities for your perceptual shifts are enormous. When you experience the living energy in all things, your connections are renewed. When you access the heart of the universe—working with energy patterns, meditation, vision, and shamanic journey—your sense of the possible expands. When you visualize the distant stars and galaxies that have been discovered by space telescopes, your dreaming ignites. When you observe the congruence of energy, spirit, and nature, worlds open; your heart connection with the heart of the universe opens.

As Star Goddess, one of my teachers, told me about finding this heart,

> *When you connect your body and cells to the heart of the universe, your whole energy changes. You are receptive to insights from the cosmic field, wisdom from what some of you call the Akashic Records. Everything changes in what you perceive, how you experience and respond, and how your cells interact with the universe. It is your free will to do this or not. The results arise from the void, all possibility, so they aren't "known" in advance. You enter into the great mystery ... the enigma, the sacred wisdom.* [8]

A BRIEF HISTORY OF ENERGY HEALING IN THE WEST

Groundwork for the revival of energy healing in the West began to be laid thirty years ago with books like Barbara Brennan's *Hands of Light*, Carolyn Myss's *Anatomy of the Spirit*, Donna Eden's *Energy Medicine*, and Richard Gerber's *Vibrational Medicine for the 21st Century*. Principles of energy anatomy from the Hindu chakra system, the Chinese meridian patterns, and other ancient systems were articulated in these books. Over time, the validity of energy healing, energy medicine, and energetic movement (practices such as *t'ai chi* and *qi gong*) were tied with emergent quantum principles.

Yet energy healing remained conceptual, even mystical, for all but the strongest medical intuitives and energy healers. Most books focused on an encyclopedic review of methodologies, systems, and ways to find practitioners. To learn to do energy healing, you used to have to take in a lot of information about chakras and meridians. With this book, that is no longer necessary.

The less-known Andean perception of the living energy universe was being introduced concurrently to Western seekers and travelers, primarily through three teachers: Alberto Villoldo, Juan Nuñez del Prado, and Américo Yábar. These three men followed a river of living oral tradition handed down by the Inca through two main sources: the Q'ero nation, which had been untainted by Western contact for four hundred years, and Don Benito Qoriwayman, a mystic in the valley below Cusco. This is the thread of tradition and practice I now place in your hands with this book.

In the Andean world, the living energy of all beings is central to life: releasing heavy energy, filling with lighter energy, and cosmic alignment are essential. Our ancient, cellular connection to the earth and the stars is incorporated into every level of existence.

Following this river of tradition, connection, and consciousness—the simple and profound ways of perceiving energy in the Andes—gives you a grounded, practical way to reconnect with nature and change your energy. This tradition invokes the boundless, renewing qualities of nature as the source for what you are becoming. It invites you to dissolve your constraining thoughts, transform your relationships, and step into a world of harmony and fluidity.

Perceiving yourself as an energy being embedded in an intrinsically connected universe—rather than seeing yourself as an isolated physical being in a finite world—opens many possibilities. Buddhist monk and teacher Thich Nat Hanh tells us,

> We want to be connected. That is the meaning of love, to be at one. When you love someone you want to say I need you, I take refuge in you. You do anything for the benefit of the Earth and the Earth will do anything for your wellbeing.[9]

EXPANDING YOUR CONNECTION WITH NATURE AND COSMOS

Your body "knows" connection with nature when you hike, garden, watch the moon rise, or collect stones and shells. Your heart remembers your own and your children's joy in climbing trees, swimming in creeks, catching polliwogs.

Yet you've mostly forgotten how to sustain your relations with mountains and trees from day to day. You may be culturally hesitant, being drawn to indigenous people but not fully believing you are a relative of earth and sky, deer and snake, mosquito and fish.

Even when you love the earth, your personal and cultural separation from nature can be a major source of dissonance and alienation.[10] Yet there's hope. When you work with intent and focus to strengthen your connections and repair what's broken—just as in any relationship—you will become empowered and energized.

In developing a relationship with a specific creature, plant, or place in nature—using your experience and direct perception rather than your ideas about something—you experience the world differently, with deepening intimacy. You nurture your sense of wonder, becoming re-enchanted with nature. In building a relationship over time, you open yourself to deep conversation. The aliveness of the land engages with you. Your compassion, empathy, and heart connections expand. Blending nature (the physical) and spirit (the mystical) together, you develop filaments of connection that weave into your life in mysterious ways.

When you develop relationships in nature, you start with where you are. You might start with a single tree in the neighborhood, a city park, a creek or a boulder, a hillock or a prairie. It might be a place in your imagination, one you've visited or wish you could visit.

The point is to learn how to connect and exchange energy with the other living beings who have inhabited this planet for 3.5 billion years: who else has this track record of wisdom and survival?

You spend every day of your life on the earth; she's always with you. When you develop a relationship with the earth and her creatures, you are never alone.

CONNECTING WITH OTHERS

Quantum physics tells us that if we change the behavior of one particle, another particle in a different location will instantaneously react, whether it's inches or universes away. It is the same with energy.

Through your energy, you are connected with all other living beings. Through your energy, you are connected outside time/space with all other weavers of the web—trees, mushrooms, clouds, whales, humans—from all spiritual traditions.

This web of connections supports you and affects you. All the parts interact with and affect the whole. The sum is much more than the parts.

When you allow yourself to experience this wholeness and inter-connectedness of living energy, your perception of everything changes. Your heart resonates.

The more you engage in global action, global meditation, and global energy shifting with others, the more you will mirror the "hundredth monkey" effect: once a hundred monkeys learn something new, the whole species "knows" without being taught. This is how we will collectively help change the world we live in.

DEVELOPING YOUR INTERNAL AUTHORITY: YOU ARE THE ONE YOU'VE BEEN WAITING FOR

To dream a new design for yourself and our world, you have to believe in your internal authority. That means breaking out of mental ideas and concepts to trust your experience, your perception, and what your heart and gut tell you. That means acting on what you know to be true, rather than holding back because someone says there's no "proof."

In a culture dominated by top-down, do-not-think-for-yourself strictures, you have to find and release a lot of unconscious assumptions, replacing them with other kinds of energy that feed your internal courage, confidence, and compassion. Such self-empowerment helps you to be and act in ways that honor the heart. It increases your spiritual competence, what you might call "inner divinity" or "spiritual muscle." It grounds you in yourself so you can connect with others in confidence and ease, sharing your special, unique qualities with the rest of us.

Such dreaming, particularly dreaming that incorporates attitude and behavioral shifts, is a huge challenge. As Rudolf Bahro writes,

"When the forms of an old culture are dying, the new culture is created by a few people who are not afraid to be insecure."[11]

WORKING WITH YOUR ENERGY, AWARENESS, AND PERCEPTION

Changing or shifting energy involves letting go of what does not serve you, connecting and filling with something else, opening your heart, developing your perception, and expanding your awareness. There is a simple, easy-to-remember pattern for this process: *Release. Connect. Fill. Open. Practice.*

This pattern threads throughout the book. *Living in the Heart of the Universe* offers practical, embodied ways to move and shift your own energy, along with eighty-four practices and meditations for deepening your energetic connections with all living beings. You will learn by doing that "where your attention goes, your energy flows."

WHAT IS PERCEPTION?

Perception describes the way you organize, identify, and interpret sensory information. Your perceptual framework allows you to take in information—or filter it out. It is largely controlled by your belief system. *In general, you do not perceive or experience things you do not think are possible.*

It is very important to understand this dynamic when you want to effect change. It is essential when you want to engage with the living beings that surround and inform you.

Looking out my windows at the oak woodland that surrounds my house one morning, I had a visceral insight: looking *at* trees is different from being *with* them. When I shifted my center of seeing from my eyes to my heart, my whole experience changed. Looking from my eyes, I experienced a separation, a kind of barrier between me and the trees; looking from my heart, I was a part of the woodland, the ecosystem. You can try this yourself.

It brought home to me once again the importance of heart and of energetic experience. Though I had been hearing about the difference between conceptual thought and perception from my teachers for a long time, it was this moment that truly shifted my understanding: true perception comes from the heart. Even after I had this insight, it took a lot of practice to stop looking at the natural world (it as separate from me) and retrain myself to see from my heart (me as a part of the whole).

YOUR PERCEPTIONS CREATE YOUR REALITY

Your perceptions generally occur automatically, outside your conscious awareness. If you believe that trees are resources to be used for building materials and paper, it is unlikely that you'll perceive the sentience and wisdom of a tree. It is unlikely that you'll believe, as the Waitaha people of New Zealand do, that "Trees are living hands, joining the Earth and the Cosmos."[12]

If your experience tells you that life is cruel, you may continually perceive suffering rather than being able to taste happiness. If your early experiences tell you that you are loved, you will probably continue to experience and perceive yourself and others as lovable.

Your perception is also affected by your expectations, your motivational state or intent, your emotional state, and your personality. If you expect to be supported and appreciated within a group, and past experience confirms that possibility, you are far more likely to perceive supportive experiences and ignore or brush off unsupportive ones. If you have an aggressive personality, you will be quick to identify aggressive words or situations.[13] In other words, your perceptions create your reality.

When you hold on to your emotional responses to an event, your body memorizes them; they become imprinted in your field. The longer they stay, the more deeply they are held and the stronger their effect on your subsequent health, emotions, and expectations. Your habits are held 95 percent in your body and only 5 percent in your mind.[14] So every change of intent, every affirmation, requires that you "unmemorize" any emotions acting as barriers and replace them with different experiences, resulting in a different emotion.

Think of most children: lacking filters between mind and heart, they are free spirits, exploring the world without the barriers of thought. When a child comes to a tree, she naturally climbs it, plays on it, dreams in it, and makes it the center of her adventures. Children imagine whatever world they want; the living energy of trees, plants, and fairies encircles them. Their perception is different because, if they are lucky, they explore the world without the barriers of rules or adult ideas.

Becoming like a child, you can change your perceptual framework by allowing the energetic, imaginative, mythic, and spiritual aspects of your experience into your awareness. As Sandra Ingerman writes,

> We used to believe that there was a physics of the large and a physics of the small. We now understand: the laws of the quantum world are applicable to the world at large, the great big world of visible matter. Those laws suggest that the observer has an effect on reality. And there is evidence that our thoughts have the capacity to change physical matter. That being the case, we have to rethink almost everything, because we've perceived a world based on separation, but the world that we're discovering now is a world of unity, where all things are fundamentally connected at the subatomic level.[15]

In "rethinking almost everything," the "four pillars of perception"—*intent, alignment, reciprocity,* and *receptivity*—will help you develop and reorganize your perception. These four qualities will help you expand your sense of interconnection, experience the effects of the "unseen," and shift your consciousness into energetic resonance: into the heart of the universe.

SHIFTING YOUR PERCEPTION AND REFRAMING YOUR STORY

Working with your energy to release the old and fill with something new helps you change your perception. Moving your energy in new directions is a way of diverting the repetitive tapes you run and the stories you tell yourself. Shifting energy is easier and more effective than working with your mind.

For many Westerners, who are conditioned to be conceptual, this may be counterintuitive. We spend a lot of time in therapy (and with our friends) talking about what happened and who did what to us. Every time we repeat the story, we embed it more deeply in our bodies; we cement the emotions we connect to our experience. When we have another, similar experience, our bodies automatically draw on our previous emotions and apply them.

For example, let's say a child has parents who expect a lot from him. When he gets a "B" in a class or only hits a single at his softball game, they say, "You could have done better" rather than "Great job!" Hearing these responses again and again, the child grows up feeling like he's not good enough, or that he can never please anyone. Naturally, these emotions are stored in his body. When his boss asks him to change part of a report he's written, the boy-man's body remembers not-good-enough, and he thinks, "Oh, the boss doesn't like my work," even though the boss really only asked for a change. This emotional perception may morph into "I'll never get a raise" and more misery for the boy-man. When he goes home and his wife asks him for the fourth time to take out the garbage, the boy-man may explode with rage: *again* he's not enough. He'll blame the wife, as she says, befuddled, "But I just asked you to take out the garbage!" Every time the boy-man brings this story, his stored emotion, into the present, he reinforces his old perception, feels lonely and separate, and deepens the divide between his reality and what others are saying and doing.

This experience, or one like it, is deeply familiar to all of us. Even when you have managed to figure out the root emotional responses that you bring to the world, even when you "know" and "understand" the dynamics that affect you, it is a continual challenge to change the dynamics. It is a continual challenge to shift into a different perspective—reframing your story—so your emotional response can match the actual situation.

Trying, practicing, and imprinting energy-shifting practices, so you can use them automatically in times of stress, are central to shifting your perception and reframing your story.

CHANGING YOURSELF, CHANGING THE WORLD

As I was writing this book, my spirit guide Apuchin told me,

> *You humans are going to have to relearn and reinvigorate your connections with each other and all living beings for your survival. You spend way too much time feeling sorry for yourselves and spinning your wheels with worry ... remember that you receive wisdom, knowing, information, and guidance through your cells, through your experience, and through your bodies. You are connected with the living energy of all, including the unseen.*

This book focuses on guiding you into *noetic, direct, experiential connections with the living universe.* The more you use your capability to be in touch with the universe you come from, as Deepak Chopra says, "... the more we will be able to heal ourselves and at the same time heal our planet. We are an integral part of a living and intelligent universe."[16] We need this connection and partnership for our survival.

Think of this book as your reference for engaging with the energy of the world. As you explore the path of energy practices, you will learn to perceive yourself as a connected, radiant being who moves and acts from your internal authority.

You will learn to see with your heart. Because ancient, indigenous, and shamanic peoples knew this, and their wisdom is reflected here, you can learn from their ways.

You will move away from isolation—and feed your profound interconnection with all beings—as you learn to sense and see living energy around you and within you.

You will shift your perception with practices of alignment, reciprocity, receptivity, and intent.

You will begin to experience unity consciousness, an embodied feeling of oneness, finding your own heart's resonance with the heart of the universe.

These are the threads and connections that will carry you into the future. Your openness allows perception. It leads to manifestation. It draws on your innate ability to transform, transmute, and become.

Portals of Possibility: How This Book Is Organized

This book is organized so you can move through it sequentially, exploring energy patterns and practices as you go. Expanding your connections with earth and the cosmos flows naturally from most of the energy-moving practices. Practices to renew your heart connections are woven throughout the book.

In chapter 1 you will enter the realm of mystical visions, sacred places, and the living energy cosmology of the Q'ero people that opened the doors of perception and connection for me. Then, in chapter 2, you begin your own energetic transformation using the central pattern of Energy Alchemy—*Release. Connect. Fill. Open. Practice.* You will learn simple practices for changing your energy by connecting with the four elements earth, air, fire, and water. You will be introduced to the "joy-body" as an alternative to the pain we so often focus on.

Chapter 3 covers the first step in Energy Alchemy: releasing. Here you will learn ways to release habits, attitudes, and emotions that are weighing you down and replace them with lighter energy. You will learn to let go of heavy energy, make compost of it, and calm your nervous system.

Then it's time for the remaining three steps of Energy Alchemy: connecting, filling, and opening. Chapter 4 explores these via the three body centers—belly, heart, and third eye, representing power, love, and vision.

The stories we tell about ourselves define "reality." Chapter 5 guides you in reframing your stories and using simple practices to change your perception.

Building on earlier practices, chapter 6 teaches you how to move through your life like a river moves through the landscape. It guides you into somatic, energetic experiences that are supportive of who you are, using a range of practices —including a central and profound energetic meditation with the elements—for deepening your connections and moving your energy.

Chapter 7 adds visualization to your sensate, heartful, imaginative connections, offering new ways to experience the alive, pusating energy in all things.

In chapter 8 you will meet again the filaments of connection that opened this introduction. Developing connective filaments with places you love is an essential way to expand your sense of interbeing. This chapter guides you in a step-by-step practice of meditating with the earth and the cosmos, a key practice for shifting vibration and anchoring in the times to come.

Chapter 9 takes you on a deeply rewarding and mystical journey, offering ways to engage and connect with the matrix of living energy. This chapter explores reciprocity, deep listening, and energy exchange with trees as ways of expanding.

Sound, meditation, and silence are the topics of chapter 10. Your own words, vibrations, and sounds affect your body, the fields around you, and the world. This chapter guides you in reflecting on and using the vibrations of sound, breath, movement, and silence to release the heavy, bring in the light, expand your connection, and shift the energy you emit.

Chapter 11 gets to the heart of transforming your body, spirit, psyche, and habits. Here you will find ways to establish daily practices for balance, concentration, and energetic protection, and address the challenges of distraction, habit, and choice.

Chapter 12 introduces you to the first of the four pillars of perceptual change I mentioned earlier in the introduction: intent. Here you will learn that intent comes from your three centers and your essence rather than from your thoughts. You will be guided in developing your intent as a means of changing your perception and experience of the problems in your life.

The second pillar of perceptual change, alignment, is the subject of chapter 13. This chapter offers numerous reasons to develop alignment and practices to stay in resonance internally and externally.

Reciprocity, the third pillar, is next: a feeling born from your heart, flowing from the cosmos and from love; it changes everything. Chapter 14 explores this sacred energy exchange from the perspective of both indigenous wisdom keepers and nature herself. It guides you in personal and group practices to experience the transformative power of reciprocity.

Chapter 15 rounds out the discussion of the four pillars by exploring receptivity. Unless you can receive love and gratitude, you cannot fully give them to others. This chapter explores the importance of receiving—and being receptive to—the gifts you are given. It discusses how belief, disbelief, confusion, and dualistic thinking can impede your receptivity, and how to move beyond those impediments.

Chapter 16 reminds you of how far you have come. It invites you to continue to perceive and engage with the filaments of connection that surround you as you weave the heart of the universe into your life.

A Weaving of Pathways

This book lends itself to a variety of approaches, depending on the areas you are most attracted to. If you are especially interested in practical, embodied ways to move and shift your energy, begin with the foundational chapters, 1 through 4. Then continue to develop your energy shifting practices with chapters 6, 9, 10, and 11.

If you are especially curious about shifting your attention and perception, I recommend you focus on chapters 5, 7, 8, and 11 through 15.

If you are most interested in deepening your connections with nature, you can begin with chapter 1 and proceed to chapters 4, 6, 7, 8, and 9.

Of course, you can move through the book just as I wrote it, a chapter at a time in sequence, or you can take your own meandering path wherever your curiosity leads.

As you learn to shift your energy, there are many threads you can follow. Taking away even just one practice from the book—deeply learned, automatic, always available to you in times of stress—is one thread to explore. Changing your energy to change your life is another.

Finding resonance with ancient, indigenous ways of perceiving the cosmos is a third thread, or filament. Reconnecting with the heart of the universe, a cosmos where all living beings are connected, is yet another.

Dreaming a society where we humans and other creatures live in resonance, attuned to each other's deepest selves, is a more mystical thread on this path. Living your deepest potential in this resonant, vibrant world—forming connections of trust, heart, and reciprocity in all your endeavors—you will change and the whole world will change with you.

May you enjoy and discover deep resonance as you weave your way on this ancient path!

Chapter 1
Changing Your Energy: The Potential

Imagine letting go of your stuck, heavy energy and releasing it so you feel lighter, more radiant, more connected. Imagine being supported as you shift into your heart, opening to the beautiful world around you. Imagine transforming your challenges—relationship, life path, financial, or physical—by learning to shift your energetic response to them. This is the potential that changing your energy—Energy Alchemy—offers you.

Challenge and Transformation

The cumulative effects of ten years spent as a single mom—sandwiched between aging alcoholic parents and an unusually challenged child—flooded over me. I couldn't breathe. I felt like I was drowning in sorrow and could never rise for air.

Overhearing another mother brag about her daughter's accomplishments—playing the violin, taking dance, and volunteering at the local humane society—shook me out of my pretense. It was a minor incident, an infinitesimal moment of shock and realization, but it was transformational for me. I understood that no matter how hard I tried, or what I did, my daughter was not like the others and our lives would never be "normal."

Like so many people who run the same tapes in their heads repeatedly, I wasn't finding solutions. I was emotionally stuck, and rarely at ease. I felt desperate and overwhelmed. I had tried many things, as you may have: meditation, therapy, exercise, journal writing, yoga, a vision quest. I had developed some insight and calmness, but I remained the same person—with the same heavy heart, challenges, and worries. As a friend observed to me, "You carry the world on your shoulders." And I can tell you: carrying the world is a pretty heavy burden!

Then one evening I heard a pivotal question: "If you have energy that's sad, why not transform it into lighter energy?"

What a concept. The speaker, a Peruvian from the high Andes, was known as a "master of moving energy." Américo Yábar was also a mystic on a mission: to bring the long-protected wisdom of the Q'ero nation to the West.

I felt him speaking directly to my heart. I had never been around anyone who was so lively and compassionate at the same time, so compelling and fervent in his vision. The picture he painted—of connecting with nature and the cosmos, shifting from head to heart, and moving our energy with fluidity—simply drew me in.

Although not a workshop-taking person, I signed up for a weekend with Américo to explore the Andean ways of using stones and ceremony (yes, I love those things). Surprising myself, a scant seven months later I traveled to Peru to experience for myself the world and the "living energy universe" he spoke of.

In the Andes, I observed that letting go of what weighs you down—hunger, worry over a sick child, a bitterly cold winter, a heavy heart—is as normal as breathing. The joy and laughter people exude is palpable and omnipresent: their habit of filling with lighter energy—cleansing winds from the mountaintops, a brilliant night sky, the companionship of other villagers—continually shifts their perception.

The Q'ero and other Quechua-speaking people I met could have perceived their lives with deep sorrow. They lived in stone huts at fifteen thousand feet. They had none of our material resources: no electricity, no vehicles, a subsistence economy. Their children were often malnourished. Their crops and herds were completely subject to the whims of nature; there were no government rescue handouts.

The itinerant doctor passed through maybe once a month. Yet they maintained their presence and joy.

Experiencing a world in which people are radiant no matter what their challenges, I wanted to figure out how they did it. What was their secret to being so joyful?

I wanted to be able to get rid of my heavy energy, or *hucha*[1] —the equivalent of getting rid of what we Westerners call neuroses and depression—as they did, and figure out how to do it every day. I didn't know it then, but as I learned to change my energy, exchanging the heavy for the lighter, I was also going to learn how to perceive life differently. I would learn to carry the world in my heart rather than on my shoulders. This changed my life. And I hope it will change yours.

THE ANDEAN COSMOVISION: TRANSFORMATIVE MOMENTS

Every culture has a way of experiencing reality, a worldview of shared values, perceptions, and principles. Referred to as *cosmovision* in South America, the Andean worldview is not abstract: it describes people's direct experience of the cosmos—ways of living in and perceiving the earth, the cosmos, and all that lies between—grounded in daily experience.[2]

In the Andean Quechua world, the living energy of all things is like breath: people exist in physical, spiritual, and engaged interconnection with stones and stars, animals and plants, earth, water, and wind—with everything. Within this cosmovision, the exchange of energy between all beings is central to keeping the collective (the world) in balance.

I found this fascinating. It connected with my deepest childhood sense of the universe as well as my adult yearning for connection. I began to immerse myself, taking two trips to the Andes and many workshops with Américo over a two-year period.

After that, I ran into another problem you may also have experienced: the gap between the ecstasy of workshop-and-travel immersion and the laundry of daily life. I had experienced a stimulating and inspiring teacher, a feeling of community and connection with like-minded souls, deep resonance with the mountains and land, and wonderful guidance in transformational experiences. Then I was back home. The demands of work, family, and life kept taking over. The frustration—of being isolated (my work mates certainly didn't want to hear about my mystical experiences), too tired to continue doing the practices I'd learned, and weighed down with a heavy heart—returned. Sound familiar?

Knowing that practice makes perfect, I determined to continually reimmerse myself in the Andean cosmovision. I poured over my own journal, workshop notes, conversations, and the few books available then. My ongoing question was "How can I incorporate this world-view into my urban-suburban life filled with buildings, machines, and technology?"

I kept asking, "How can I stay connected with the earth and the cosmos?" "How can I shift my energy from heavy to light?" "How can I become more joyful?" As I reexperienced and revisited my many trans-formative experiences in the Andes, they guided me toward deeper understanding of the "how."

One such experience had occurred when our small group of trav-elers walked down a steep trail from the village of Mollomarca to the wild river called Mapacho Mayu. We passed a shy couple guiding an ox yoked to a single-furrow plow, breaking up the rich red soil for planting. On the river's banks, we became aware of harmony among the elements: wind from the jungle, water from the mountains, heat from the sun, earth beneath our feet. Instructed to do a meditation, this was my experience:

I reflect on Ausangate, the source of this river. The Mapacho Mayu begins with ice melt from the sacred mountain: drip, drip, drip—form-ing rivulets, then creeks, then smaller rivers flowing into larger ones. The river grows with rain runoff and snowmelt, flowing down into the Amazon basin; many other rivers join with it to form the Amazon river-sea. Along all the rivers, water evaporates, creating a biosphere of moisture. Water returns to air, cloud, rain, cycling over and over. In this weaving of water, each drop counts, is a part of the whole.

This is the important message: "Each drop of water counts." Each consciously action, each meditation, each cleansing, each filament of connection is like a drop of water contributing to the web you weave in your life.

This meditation exemplifies the connection that is woven into the Andean world: with the four elements, the surrounding natural world, the cosmos—with the energy that animates the universe. This life force, a main organizing principle of the cosmovision, became another focus of inquiry: "How can I experience, feel, know this living energy?"

A second transformative moment had occurred during a cleansing-and-protection ritual. When it was my turn for a healing, Doña Felicitas Q'awaña, the elder shaman, placed my foot on a straw cross (*Tiwantisuyu*, the four directions) and tied handspun yarn around my left big toe. She slowly wrapped it around my body, moving to her left, chanting. Breaking the yarn above my head, and still moving to her left, she continued to break the yarn at each of the crossing points (third eye, heart, belly). I felt one of the blockages in my heart break open, with a sensation of fresh air rushing in.

When everyone was cleansed, the assistant shaman, Maria, gathered all the yarn and left the room. We were told that she ran quickly to the creek, offering the broken threads with her left hand to the water, which carried them to the sea. There, mother ocean (*Mamacocha*, the original source of feminine energy) would receive, "eat," and transform them.

Though simple in outward form, this *lloq'e nacuy* healing is embedded with profound layers of meaning. The intent is to neutralize, heal, and transform heavy energy and open the person to the "undomesticated" (*salk'a*) fluid aspects of life. This is what happened when I felt my heart "break open." Winding the body with yarn, the shaman's intent is to connect the person's filaments with the light of the stars, the upper world (*hanaq'pacha*). As she breaks your filaments of heavy energy—pain, sadness, depression, envy—the "lighter" filaments of your etheric body and those of Mother Earth (*Pachamama*) rise up and mingle with the filaments of the stars and the upper world, creating feelings of being cleansed, energized, peaceful, filled, and rejuvenated. Inside reflects outside: belly, heart, and the third eye of the forehead correspond with the three spiritual worlds—lower, middle, and upper—traditional to shamanic cultures worldwide.

I was deeply moved by the power of unbroken spiritual lineage in this ceremony. Having endured the Spanish conquest, and in spite of it, people in the high Andes have retained ritual, prophecy, and meaning from pre-Incan times. I felt empowered by the bridges that connect us all through time and space, yet my ever-present question arose: How can I translate this into my world?

BECOMING A BRIDGE BETWEEN CULTURES

I had been asking "how" and finding practices to translate the Andean vision into my own for some years when I took another trip to Peru. At the foot of a shrinking glacier at Qoylloriti, our group gathered in ceremony with Q'ero teachers and other *paqos* (mystics and healers). We had hiked together to nearly 16,000 feet to reach this sacred place. Making offerings to the spirits of the land and waters, the mountains and stones, we wove our personal intent into the communal *despacho*, a beautiful, ancient, and traditional offering ceremony.[3]

As part of the ceremony, I was gifted with a dense, smooth, slightly curved, heavy gray stone.[4] As the stone nestled in my hand, the word "bridge" (*chacaruna*) popped into my awareness. I understood that my long personal integration of Andean cosmovision, and my perception of living energy in all things, was taking a leap. I was to be a bridge between the cultures of the North and the South, joining a long tradition of those who walk what is known as the rainbow bridge (*k'uychi chaka*).[5] Unbeknownst to me in that moment, at that ceremony, and in that sacred place, the threads of this book began to weave themselves together.

RECIPROCAL RELATIONSHIPS

When you engage with spirit, with the living energy in all things, your reciprocity circles back around to you. As shamanic cultures around the world say, when you make a relationship with mountain or tree, river or wind, the living energy of that being reciprocates and begins to teach you. The mountain dreams you and supports you when you walk her flanks and honor her in ceremony. When you maintain the forest, the forest breathes you, exhaling oxygen to support all life on the planet. When you tend your flower and vegetable gardens, the plants nourish you with food, beauty, and connection. When you keep the ecosystem whole and intact, it offers you the sublime diversity of animals, insects, plants, and energy in balance. This is the balance that supports all life, the balance that indigenous peoples weave their lives around.

In indigenous and close-to-the-land cultures, those for which everything is alive and exists in relationship, energy is the framework and focus of life. Humans are fully integrated and at one with the natural environment, the world of living energies, and the world of spirit. Living in reciprocity with all beings is essential for receiving guidance, information, and teaching from the healing plant or the sacred mountain. Such wisdom is experienced as valid, reliable, essential knowledge.

This is the wisdom you will learn to access in this book: living in reciprocity and connection with all of life.

Premise and Promise: Where Your Attention Goes, Your Energy Flows

In the Andes the past is perceived as ahead of us, and future behind us—mysterious, hidden, not yet known. As Eric Pearl writes, admitting that we do not know the answers opens potentials and possibilities to us. Not knowing lets us observe. Experiencing without judgment allows new wisdom to come through, and "points us towards . . . our natural state of connection."[6]

We have stepped fully into the time for "dreaming a new dream" for ourselves and for the planet. We have passed through the 2012 galactic shift into a new fifty-six-thousand-year cycle, prophesied as a time of great potential by indigenous wisdom keepers worldwide.

No matter what challenges you face, you can always view them through a different lens. This book's lens is energy.

To help you dream your own new dream, this book guides you in exploring simple patterns and practices for changing your energy.

When you view everything as just energy, there's no judgment. You can learn to *notice* energy that no longer serves you and *release* it. You can *connect* and *fill* with something lighter. You can *open* to the beautiful world of living energy that surrounds you: this takes you outside of your small self, beyond the ego, and reconnects you with the great web. You can open to "the environment as your extended body," as Deepak Chopra puts it. You can cultivate your *perception* and energetic relationship with other living beings by developing your intent, alignment, reciprocity, and receptivity.

The choices you have with your attention and energy are illustrated by an old Apache story:

> *A grandfather is teaching his grandson about life. "A fight is going on inside me," he says. "It is a terrible fight between two wolves. One wolf is angry, arrogant, resentful, and judgmental. The other wolf is kind, compassionate, and generous. Sometimes it is hard to live with these two wolves inside me, for both try to dominate my spirit. The same happens for you and everyone."*
>
> *The grandson thinks for a minute, then asks, "Who will win?"*
>
> *His grandfather replies, "The wolf you feed."* [7]

If you feed the wolf of compassion and kindness, your energy moves in that direction. If you focus your attention on being open hearted, your energy moves in that direction. Conversely, if you focus on the heavy or negative aspects of your experience—in your behavior, the stories you tell, or the chatter in your mind—your energy remains stuck there.

Move Your Energy

To help you focus your attention and move your energy, simple patterns of energy awareness, connection, practice, and perception thread throughout the book. The effects these patterns have had on my relationships, my view of the world, and my path have been profound. The transformative power for my students has been equally rich. My intent now is to share the essence and depth of this work with you.

Playing with energy is a game and a dance. As you explore the patterns of the dance, which are woven into eighty-four practices, you will find what works for you. As I have, you will learn to:

- Shift from the heaviness in your life—problems, worry, sadness, and suffering—into the beauty of connection with all that is.
- Replace your self-doubt, disconnection, and isolation with vitality and joy as you develop your energetic connection with the earth and the whole cosmos.
- Change your perceptions of relationships, responsibilities, and "reality" itself by developing your intent, receptivity, reciprocity, and alignment.
- Experience the power of moving your energy from one state to another, and learn to maintain your own harmony, balance, and connection.
- Find and conduct your life from your truth, your beauty, and your true essence.
- Deepen your energetic connection with all living beings, the earth that supports you, and the cosmos that birthed you, ending your sense of separation.

The beauty of these energy patterns and practices is that they are easy to learn. They have been used for a very long time with cumulative and deepening effects. You can do them for yourself as often as you want. With repetition, they help you see how to shift your emotions, your actions, and your perceptions in minutes.

CHANGE YOUR PERCEPTIONS
OF WHAT WEIGHS YOU DOWN

What you explore in this book will not change your problems directly. It will change your experience and perception of whatever weighs you down: you will be able to leave behind assumptions, paradigms, and cultural beliefs that currently control you. You will shift away from isolating individualism and disconnection from nature, moving toward a more communal, collective, global awareness. You will see and experience yourself in resonance with all beings. Uncovering who you were born to be, you will live a more joyous, purposeful, authentic life, imagining a different world into being and living ever more in harmony with the planet. You will, in the words of the Q'ero, "be connected with everything."

This deep transformation begins for you now. In the next chapter you will learn the essential pattern of Energy Alchemy. You will be introduced to simple practices for shifting your energy, and the importance of breath, intent, and energy awareness in building your joy-body.

Chapter 2
Energy Alchemy:
Basic Patterns

Being connected with everything sounds good, doesn't it?

Yet it may be hard to imagine. Your heart has been hurt in connection, or your mind tells you that it is not possible. Your body may resist with caution, or even fear. Your isolation sometimes overwhelms you.

This is why working with your energy—releasing what no longer serves you and filling with something lighter—can be so transformative. Energy Alchemy sidesteps your thoughts, beliefs, emotions, and mental constructs. It helps you experience directly.

Energy Alchemy draws on ancient wisdom and practices: though it is not commonly known in the Western world, you're not starting from scratch. If you are among those for whom therapy, affirmations, coaching, or other modalities haven't resulted in long-term success, Energy Alchemy will help you step away from your intractable problems and into joyful connection.

Understanding Energy Alchemy

The essence of Energy Alchemy is transformation. Instead of transmuting base metals into gold as the alchemists in the Middle Ages tried to do, you learn to transmute your heavy, dense energy into lighter, more nurturing energy. Changing your energy changes your life.

Everything in the universe exchanges energy. Massive stars collapse and form black holes. Seeds sprout, grow, fruit, and decompose to feed new growth. What falls apart becomes source energy for what is becoming—in us, in seeds, in stars.

The essential pattern of Energy Alchemy is a simple exchange. You *release* energy that no longer serves you, and *fill* with lighter energy. By exchanging the heaviness inside you for the lighter, living energy of a plant, a gentle breeze, or any other living being, you replace separation with connection.

Practicing Energy Alchemy helps you cultivate the power, untapped potential, and resonance of your energy body. It lets you step into the largest story you are capable of living, moving beyond your "small self" into connection with all the living beings around you.

When you view everything as simply energy, there's no judgment. There's no positive or negative: it is just energy, transforming. Understanding the pattern of energy exchange, and the principles and assumptions that underlie it, is very helpful in engaging easily with the nature-based practices in this book.

RELEASING AND FILLING: EXPERIENCING FLUIDITY

The underlying principle of all energetic releasing and filling is that lower frequencies (heavier, denser, disordered energy) attune to higher frequencies (lighter, more refined, more harmonious energy). By consciously releasing the heavy and filling with the light, you can shift your spirit, body, mind, and energy field. You learn energetic fluidity—switching from sadness to equanimity, for instance, or from burnout to openheartedness—as you embody the process.

You have likely experienced energetic fluidity if you have ever practiced gratitude. When you concentrate on being grateful—an emotion that fills your heart with joy and light—you resonate with your own appreciation. Irritations and fatigue dissipate; you feel better. In other words, the more refined energy of gratitude trumps the denser, heavier feelings you started with.

Similarly, you probably feel much happier when you are in nature than when you are in the middle of a factory or office building: the density of energy in the office makes you feel heavy; the lightness of trees and wind and water lightens your mood.

When you are drawn to an ancient sacred site, you are feeling the energetic fluidity and lightness of reverence, ceremony, and beauty that is held there. When you are drawn to a great spiritual teacher, her presence elicits your own energetic, embodied resonance and attunement.

Energetic releasing and filling is also based on the reality of your interconnections: you are affected by and pick up energy from the people around you and from events in the world.

Even when your personal life is going fine, you pick up "stuff." In the world beyond your personal dramas, what is happening dribbles into your energy field, muddies the view, or acts like blobs of debris, making things harder and heavier. As changes in the world speed up, you find yourself working harder to stay clear, clean, and open. Energetic releasing and filling can be applied to all energy, no matter where it comes from.

Just as your body releases the vivid memories of breaking a leg, giving birth, or having surgery—retaining only a memory or idea that it hurt—you can learn to release emotional pain and fill with something new.

CONNECTING AND OPENING

Learning to keep your energy body clear and light is key to being present and empowered. Whether you are facing a partner's rage, a disaster, a child's disappointment, or the state of the earth, Energy Alchemy helps you be as openhearted and filled with your natural radiance as possible.

In this state, you can support others, be loving, and affect energy fields beyond your own.

Dense, heavy energy comes from human responses: greed, anger, hatred, jealousy, shame, blame, and all those other emotions that create separation. Whether it's because someone else is angry and you feel like running from the room, or because you are hurt and you blame the other, you automatically feel separate. The longer this goes on, the harder it is to overcome this feeling.

Reconnecting with and opening to the light, nonjudgmental energy of your natural surroundings replaces the density of human reaction.

When you connect more strongly and surely with any part of nature—trees, creatures, rivers, or the earth herself—you clear the debris that surrounds you and move more surely from your essence. In feeling, experiencing, and perceiving your interconnections, you expand and open your heart to the world as it is. In compassion, you can let rage and despair arise, and fall away. You can let sadness arise, and fall away. You can let go of judgment (who is bad, who is good) and just be with what is. You can experience interbeing, the sense that you are a part of everything and everything is a part of you. As Buddhist teacher Sharon Salzberg says,

> *Compassion is the trembling or the quivering of the heart in response to suffering. Equanimity is a spacious stillness that can accept things as they are. The balance of compassion and equanimity allows us to profoundly care, and yet not get overwhelmed and unable to cope with that caring.* [1]

The practices of releasing, connecting, filling, and opening—practices you will explore throughout the book—will help you find equanimity and compassion. They will help you act from a place of power. As you experience interbeing, you will shift the energy in the world.

BREATHING

Breathing is an incredible ally in your effort to be present, relieve stress, and live from your essence. When you breathe deeply, evenly, and with awareness—as you do in any physical exercise class—your body fills with freshness.[2] Your cells fill with *prana* and *qi*. You feel your natural rhythms return to an easy flow and exchange. Your energy becomes like your breath, deep and easy. Resistances and blockages dissipate, allowing you to draw in the beauty all around you.

As you will learn, conscious breathing is central to all releasing and filling practices, just as it is central to meditation, dance, yoga, qi gong, Pilates, singing, toning, and every other practice that involves focus, concentration, and observation. Panache Desai tells us,

> *I've discovered a way to turn life into living meditation, and that is to rest in the awareness of your breath. Just simply observe your inhalation and exhalation as it unfolds in each moment. The more you do that, the*

more naturally you calm down, your central nervous system calms down, you disengage from these fight or flight responses, the fear based reactions that run you ...You can then start to be peaceful in the midst of life. Resting in the awareness of your breath transforms your life into living meditation. When you are triggered, stop, slow down, and breathe. [3]

Conscious breathing calms your nervous system. It also enables you to move from one kind of activity to another. For example, when my daughter was young I wanted to shed the intense and hyper-focus of my consulting business and be present with her slower pace and energy by the time I picked her up from day care. As I drove away from my Silicon Valley clients and toward her day care, I breathed deeply along the freeway, transforming into Mom by the time I arrived.

I invite you to try this practice of conscious breathing right now. The more you embed it into your body and psyche's toolkit through practice, the more easily you'll be able to draw on conscious breathing when you need it.

BREATHING CONSCIOUSLY

Breathe in deeply, filling your lungs and belly with fresh air. Blow out all the stale air and toxins, emptying your lungs and then your belly.

Repeat three more times, focusing on feeling the air move in and out. Notice how you feel, and what happened to your thoughts, even if briefly.

INTENT

Intent includes the energetic attention, passion, spirit, and direction you choose to focus on as you move through your world. Intent arises from your whole being: your body, mind, heart, and spirit, the light and the heavy, the sunlight and the shadow. True intent takes into account your weaknesses as well as your strengths, so it doesn't set you up to fail. Acting with intent sends an energetic vibration into the world, feeding what you are trying to create—personally, politically, globally—and affects the cumulative outcome of things.

Developing your intent is central to shifting your perception, so we'll delve more deeply into intent throughout the book.

Your Energy Awareness

Being aware of your energy is your natural, human state. You'll learn about this by experiencing and exploring it.

You may wonder what your energy is, or how to feel it. You are not alone! Most of us—unless we come from a very unusual background—are trained to trust the physical, material, mental world and to question and doubt the energetic, metaphysical world. The antidote to this doubt is exploration: trying something different.

GUIDELINES FOR EXPLORING

Follow these three key guidelines as you explore:

- Try the practices; do not just read about them. They are only useful if you experience their effects.
- Ask yourself: What is my intent? What do I want to change in my life? Am I willing to follow the advice and instructions offered to me? Your intent, trust, and openness are crucial components of your energy awareness. If you are not quite sure what your intent is, for now you might try "sincere pretending," as Oakley Gordon calls it.
- Notice and observe what happens in your heart, your relationships, and your perception. Pay attention to your body's response—especially your breath, sensations, and level of muscle tension or relaxation—for clues.

As you explore and develop your energy awareness using the practices in the book, you will find yourself naturally reconnecting with the life around you. You will find it easier to move and shift your own energy in response to both personal and community challenges. Your perceptual skills will increase.

Experience and practice are key. Everyone has different skills and ways of "seeing," and we can all do it. The energy fields you live in communicate information to you all the time. Practice helps your cells remember what used to be natural to you. Your job is to experience: to open, listen, receive, share, and allow yourself to be transformed.

As Dr. Synthia Andrews writes in her book *The Path of Energy*,

Energy structures maintain the organization of your physical body, including emotions, thinking patterns, and sensations. The easiest way to change a physical pattern, whether in your body or the circumstances of your life, is to first change the configuration of your energy. [4]

DEVELOPING YOUR ENERGY AWARENESS

Here are some simple ways to develop your awareness as you explore and try the practices:

- Experiment with all five senses. We all have different sensory strengths when accessing energetic information; what one person sees, another person hears or feels. All the senses are equally valid.
- Trust your inner authority, your felt sense of an experience. For example, if you suddenly feel heaviness in your heart that makes you want to leave the room, leave it. You can figure out who or what triggered you energetically later.
- Start by choosing one practice that appeals to you. Try it for a week or more. If you experience no effects, let it go and try another.
- Try to suspend your judgment and the mental constructs that keep you tied to your old ways and beliefs.
- Shift your attention from looking at something—the trees in your neighborhood, the butterfly flitting by—to feeling yourself as a part of the forest, a relative of the butterfly.
- Use your hands to feel the energy of people, trees, and animals.

EARTH, AIR, FIRE, AND WATER: YOUR COMPANIONS

In this section you will learn the simplest, most basic practices for changing the configuration of your energy. When you have a pain, a sorrow, or anything that weighs you down, you can release it to air, water, fire, or earth and fill yourself with the energy of these elements.

Earth, air, fire, and water are alive both inside your body and outside. They make life possible. They circulate and dance in you and around you, moving and shifting the whole planet. In all the universes, everything comes from the elements: they create a unity that our spiritual consciousness can tap into. They are always present and available! As Tenzin Wangyal Rinpoche writes, "The elements are all that exists, so we can always do practice with the elements, at any time, wherever we are, whatever we are doing."[5] My local mountain spirit expresses it this way:

Observe the elements to see about moving your energy. When great winds blow through, let something go. When precious sun warms the day for a few hours, draw in the light. When it rains or snows, ask yourself what in your life you are watering and feeding. When the quiet, long dark comes, let yourself enter the womb of silence and mystery.

Air moving in your lungs is the breath of your life; wind brings rain and cleans the air. Fire warms you and transforms everything it touches; sun enables living things to grow, fruit, and flourish. Earth supports life, nourishing seeds that become the food you eat, growing the forests that provide your oxygen, and transforming physical and energetic compost into other kinds of energy. Water sustains life; it carries memory to maintain connection. We know that all earth's water came from the stars: imagine what you might learn from it, or from drinking glacier water that formed into ice ten thousand or a hundred thousand years ago, if you listen carefully!

The elements are always present, interacting with each other and affecting all your senses. They model and teach you about interrelationship and moving energy as you connect with the external element and internalize its qualities. Your intimate, constant engagement with the elements makes them perfect companions for elemental practices of releasing heaviness and bringing in the light.

One of my students described how she used the practices to address a family crisis:

My sister is an addict, and usually doesn't communicate with me. When she went into a downward spiral, a lot of my old buttons were pushed. I started releasing all my heavy and dense feelings (sadness,

*fear, anger, and loss) to the earth as often as I needed; then I'd bring
the light of the sun into my heart. Some days I'd repeat this six or eight
times. It gave me some equanimity. My feelings kept returning during
the crisis, but I didn't want to store them in my body, so I just kept at it.*

RELEASING AND FILLING WITH AIR

Breathe your heaviness out through your throat, gifting it to the air.
Breathe in the soft breeze, the wild wind, the clean air, filling your
lungs and all your cells. Keep gifting your heaviness to the air—a
delicious snack—until you feel calmer and full. Thank the air.

As you bring the element of air in, filling and connecting with its
qualities and replacing your heavy energy with lighter energy, notice
how you feel. Are you a little less isolated, feeling a little easier in your
heart? Do you feel expanded or connected with the wider world?

RELEASING AND FILLING WITH WATER

Breathe your heaviness out through your tailbone, imagining the
aquifer beneath your feet receiving it as a gift. Breathe in the wonderful fluid energy of water through your tailbone. Let it join with all
the water in your body, filling your cells and organs. Keep gifting
your heaviness to the water—a delicious snack—until you feel full
of fresh, clear running water. Thank the water.

RELEASING, FILLING,
AND OPENING TO THE SUN

You can do this anywhere, at any time. When you have an intractable
heaviness, repeating the practice throughout the day will help you shift,
slowly and surely, to lightness. Sun is fire ...

Face the sun. Open your heart, breathing out all your heavy energy
into the sun. Breathe in the heat, warmth, and transformative power of the sun.

Repeat, breathing out heavy energy and breathing in sun energy,
until your heart feels full and clear again. Thank the fire of the sun.

RELEASING AND FILLING WITH EARTH

Focus on the earth. Breathe out all your heavy energy through your belly—below your belly button, the area known as hara, dan tien, qosq'o—into the earth. Now breathe earth energy back up into your belly. Imagine the rich, fecund soil replacing the heaviness and flowing to all the organs of your body, to your bones, your cells, your skin. Repeat this until you feel full. Thank the earth.

Noticing the Differences

Most of the time I release general heaviness or density when I connect and fill with the elements. It is not necessary to identify the heaviness: in fact, it is usually better to just let it all go without trying to name the feelings.

You can, however, use the elements to release a particular weight that you have noticed. For example, one day you might be feeling sad, off center, or anxious: you can focus on that specific density and intend to release it.

I've learned over time that each element has a slightly different effect in my body. You can try this for yourself, discovering which element works best for you, playing with it and exploring it inside and out. You can also test the various elements with the same heaviness to see what works best.

I recommend starting with whichever element you like or relate to best. Your experience will help you know the element better and deepen your relationship to it. Enjoying a practice is what will help you continue doing it!

Remember, you are always exchanging energy with the elements— gifting them with your energy, receiving the gift of their energy. The elements don't have labels for emotions: our energetic compost is just energy.

Later in the book—in chapter 6—you'll learn how to work with all the elements together in the Elements Meditation.

Your Pain Body
and Your Joy Body

Almost everyone carries accumulations of old emotional pain, what Eckhart Tolle calls the "pain-body." This pain-body feeds on what has happened in the past, and associates your current pain with all similar instances of pain. This pain-body feeds on negative thinking and drama in relationships. It is often fed by ancestral as well as personal experience. It may manifest as fear, defensiveness, loneliness, or a sense of separation. The pain-body is an energy field of its own, Tolle says, with

> ... its own primitive intelligence, not unlike a cunning animal ... the food it requires to replenish itself consists of energy that is compatible with its own, which is to say, energy that vibrates at a similar frequency. Any emotionally painful experience can be used as food by the pain-body.[6]

Similarly, what I call your "joy-body" contains all the love, wonderful experiences, and associated emotions that you collect over the years. Like the pain-body, your joy-body stores family, ancestral, and collective joy. It feeds on positive, transporting experience. The importance of this to your living energy, your power to promote change in your emotional responses, and your creativity is profound. Like the grandfather feeding the wolf in chapter 1, you have a choice about what you feed, what you eat, and how you digest what comes your way.

Every meditation practice teaches that your feelings and reactions arise, then change, then change again; *your pain and mental responses are not you.* This point of view offers you freedom to move in and out of feeling states with fluidity; to change your mind; and to avoid getting stuck in those "heavy" and redundant thoughts that occupy 75 percent of your thinking.

Working with energy helps you sidestep your mental responses and redundant thoughts like "I'm not good enough," or "I'll never find a mate." It is not necessary to continually identify and label your emotions as happy, depressed, angry, harmonious, and so on (in the Buddhist view, all of our emotions and reactions are illusions). It is not necessary to tell the stories behind your feelings, or the source and cause of them, over and over again. In general, such repetition cements the energetic memories in your mind, body, and energy field, making them more challenging to shift. It also draws others to you who share similar stories. This can be comforting in the short run but entangling over time.

Even deep wounds can be released energetically. You may be more successful if you have support in this—help in identifying source and genesis, reminders to use energetic release, and guidance in learning which practices will work. (For further support, see http://www.megbeeler.com)

You *can* choose to release energetically and shift your attention away from your pain-body and toward your joy-body; however, you cannot always do this alone.

Whatever your experience, because heaviness embeds in the body and rules your "cunning animal" (limbic brain) responses, using energetic shifting to move things around has profound effects. I have experienced this in my own life. Shifting out of my own habitual suffering and poor-me perceptions, teaching clients and students how to use these energy-shifting practices and perceptions, and seeing the inner joy of Q'ero wisdom keepers in the Andes have changed my world.

IMAGINING A JOYFUL WAY

In *Awakening Joy*, James Baraz and Shoshona Alexander write

> *Joy is not for the lucky few. It's a choice anyone can make. Joy is already there inside you. It is inherent in every one of us, an innate capacity, like the ability to learn a language or to love. As innocent babies we came into this world with a natural joy, and we can discover it again.*[7]

Fluid awareness, gratefulness, and joy can become your state of mind. Imagine you and your friends focusing on each other's wonderful and joyful qualities ... Imagine relating to your family—children, partner, parents—from a place of radiance and open-heartedness ... Imagine world leaders talking about how brilliant and wonderful other leaders, religions, cultures, and countries are ...

You need not wait for the leaders; you are the one you've been waiting for.

You can notice your own thought patterns, topics of conversation, and the energies behind your words, and learn to shift the heavy doses of negativity you are used to.

You can learn to shift your focus from pain to joy.

You can learn to fill yourself with the vital energy that surrounds you.

You can visualize a peaceful, harmonious world.

You can feed your pragmatic shifts with inspiring, mystical experience.

You can set your intent to explore the universe, a potential source of refined energy, connection, and wisdom.

Practice and repetition embed transformation in your body, psyche, and habits. Noticing, releasing, filling, connecting, and opening help you move from pain-body to joy-body.

The more internally clear you become, the stronger a conduit you can be for balance, healing, and bringing light to the world. Join me in learning how in the next chapter, where you will learn how to release habits, attitudes, and emotions to make way for lighter, more joyful energy.

CHAPTER 3
PUSHING THE BOULDERS ASIDE: RELEASING HABITS, ATTITUDES, AND EMOTIONS

Your emotions and reactions, and the labels you give them, can feel like boulders in your path: big, heavy, and impossible to move. When your underlying perceptions and interpretations of events are fixed or rigid as rock, nothing can change. These boulders stand in the way of making your life and relationships more resonant, fulfilling, and joyous.

Working energetically, which entails leaving mental labels aside, lets you release dense, heavy stuff so you feel lighter, energized, and more in balance. This takes *intent* (wanting to let go) and *action* (doing a practice of energetic release).

When you learn to notice where your energy goes, you can figure out what, exactly, the boulder in your path *is*. To what emotions, thoughts, beliefs, habits, or stories do you give your attention? Is your mind clinging like Velcro to heavy boulders, small rocks—or hidden gems?

Noticing where your energy goes helps you replace habits of mind and fixed ideas about yourself that perpetuate what you think. Noticing where your energy goes also helps you replace memories stored in your body, particularly trauma and old pain. What if you could replace "no one loves me" with an inner, felt sense of being wonderful? What if you could replace "I am not good enough" with confidence in your ability to do what you set out to do? What if you could replace "I'll never get what I want" with step-by-step experiences of accomplishment?

Releasing what doesn't belong to you helps you be whole; it helps you to follow your heart, act with power, and access your wisdom. Releasing helps you flow with synchronicity. Releasing what doesn't belong to you helps you discover what does belong to you: the path to your destiny.

As visionary healer Eda Zavala says, "If you have any pain or anger in yourself, you cannot help your community. You need lighter energy!"[1] Putting this a different way, Q'ero wisdomkeeper Humberto Sonqo Quispé tells us, "Fear is something we build. Then it becomes collective. We have to release the fear."[2]

Energy practices are accumulative: the more you do, the more things change. Working with your energy contributes to both your personal healing and the healing of the world.

ENERGY BLOCKAGES

Imagine the energies you carry entangling with the emotions, reactions, difficulties, and challenges of your day. They become like small snarls in your hair, or a net caught on the rocks. Without attention, the tangles grow and worsen, blocking the smooth flow of energy that keeps you healthy on all levels. Over the years, the blockages can turn to disease. In the worst cases, your DNA coils and loses its ability to repair your cells.

With attention and intent, you can open the blockages, smooth the tangles, and bring in the healing light of the universe, allowing your natural energy flow to resume, both protecting and invigorating you.

You can get help with this because you live in an interconnected, multidimensional universe of living energy where we all (trees, water, stones, humans, butterflies, mountains) are part of one another. Moving your energy blockages (those boulders) effects physical healing by taking you into your essential self, where your cells listen and respond. As your energy body is healed, the physical cells in your body are able to shift and change as well.

In the morphic field of healing, intent plays an essential role. Your intent, trust, and openness to the process are crucial components. Ask yourself: What is my intent? What do I want to change in my life? Am I willing to move some boulders and take in something new?

THE PROCESS OF SHIFTING ENERGY: AN EXAMPLE

From time to time in this book I will use examples to help ground the ideas I share. For example, to illustrate the process you might go through to shift your energy, I'll tell you the story of a mom. This mom worked to change the dynamics between herself and her two-year-old child by moving her own energy. As you read the story, imagine you are the mom.

Step 1: Mom notices that she frequently yells in frustration at her resistant two-year-old. She tries to figure out why she gets so mad; after all, she knows that two-year-olds are notorious for saying "No!" Observing carefully, she notices that Dad often blames her for the ruckus: a double whammy. Sorting through what she's feeling—where she is putting her attention—Mom sees that she is afraid her child will get hurt, afraid she is not a good parent, and afraid she can't control the situation. She realizes that her rage is masking her fear. Her yelling is not the boulder—the fear beneath it is the boulder.

When you identify the toxic thought or behavior, you can set your intent to transmute or change its nature energetically.

Step 2: She tells herself, "Rather than being afraid, I want to be loving and openhearted." Her intent is to be and act loving with her child, even when disciplining him.

When you have awareness and intent, you can take action. Any practice of energetic release engages you with living energy and with the fields that surround you. Having emptied out the dense, you can bring in the light, focusing your attention on what nurtures and feeds you.

Step 3: Mom decides on three actions. First, she'll take a big breath and hug her two-year-old before reacting. Second, she'll use a gratitude practice. And as a backup, she'll distract her child (and herself) with a different activity, toy, or game.

Obviously, energetic shifting takes time and practice. If you are the person who has been getting mad again and again, you'll have to keep trying to shift your behavior. If one approach is too difficult, or is hard to remember, you'll have to try something else. As your body notices the difference in your feelings (big hug compared to big mad), the feelings will help you shift. In the end, you'll find it amazing how reliably intent followed by action changes your perspective and shifts your behavior!

Boulder-Releasing and Shifting Practices

Releasing does not have to be time consuming. It does help to *do it frequently*, however: by shifting your attention repeatedly, you shift your energy. Grounding, balance, and energetic protection are *really* important to pay attention to, every day.

They are so simple you can do them anytime—on your ten-minute break, at lunch, standing in line, walking around the block, in the middle of the night. They help you move through all the changes in the world with grace and compassion rather than fear and constriction.

Now it's time for you to learn how to release your boulders. What follows are quick practices you can easily incorporate into your day.

DAILY INTENDING

Start every day with "I intend to release what is not mine and no longer serves me. I intend to allow in only what is appropriate for me at this time."

Doing this before you get up in the morning helps you start your day calm and collected.

SCANNING

Scan your physical body, and then your energetic body, with your mind's eye. Release any dense or heavy-feeling stuff you notice (you do not have to identify it first!) to one of the elements of water, air, earth, or fire. Fill yourself with the energy of the same element.

In other words, if you release to water, fill with the energy of water; if you release to earth, fill with the energy of earth.

VISUALIZING

Visualize a person or place you love. Let your heart fill with whatever this invokes.

This is great for shifting your attention away from a problem. As an eighty-year-old friend of mine says, "Whenever I get too upset about the state of the environment, I look at the mountain or a tree to make myself feel better."

GIFTING A STONE

Stones and rocks are found everywhere, so it's easy to use this practice any time you take a walk. This is a nice one to teach children too, for they naturally pick up (and want to hurl) stones.

On a walk, find a stone to symbolize something you want to release, such as a heavy feeling or an issue that is bothering you. Offer the issue or feeling to the stone, asking it to take the energy of what you are releasing.

Carry the stone as you walk. As you periodically notice its weight or edges in your hand, think of what it is carrying for you. Appreciate it.

When the time is right, thank the stone and toss it far away (being careful not to hit anyone). Feel it take your heaviness as it flies through the air and back to the earth. Notice the lightness in your body; feed this lightness by breathing in fresh air and sunlight.

MAKING COMPOST OF YOUR HEAVY ENERGY

"Worry causes heavy energy. Avoid it," Q'ero Humberto Sonqo Quispé tells us.[3]

There is no positive or negative energy, only *heavy energy* and more refined, or *lighter energy*. In making compost of your heavy energy, your intent is to move the heavy, disharmonious, disordered energy out of your field and into the earth, which loves to receive. Think of your energy as part of the continual flow of living energy in the whole universe.

In this practice you will treat all the heaviness and density in your body, heart, and mind—headaches, despair, defensiveness, fear, resentments, and so on—as energetic compost. Like the physical compost from kitchen and garden waste, your energetic compost can feed the earth. What is disintegrating and falling apart becomes a source of energy for what is becoming. This is true in us, on the earth, and in the cosmos.

The beauty of *moving* energy is that you don't have to identify or name what you are releasing: It is just energy! It's like tossing a banana peel. You no longer need it, so you put it in the compost, gifting it back to the earth. Similarly, you can release your heavy energy with no judgment, without rejecting it or clinging to it.[4] As Thich Nhat Hanh says, "If we don't practice mindfulness, there is no way to transform garbage back into a flower."[5]

Remember, it takes at least as much of your energy to suppress a displeasing, disordered, or heavy feeling as it does to release it and take in something new.

EATING HEAVY ENERGY

Try doing this first composting practice once an hour, quickly. This pattern—of releasing and filling, in reciprocity—is central to learning to move your energy. In the Andes, this is called eating *hucha*: eating heavy energy.

> Imagine an opening from your belly, just below your belly button, with a channel feeding into the earth. Think of the channel as an energetic stomach. You intend to let the heaviness flow out from you through this channel. You intend to feed the earth with your wonderful compost, joyfully letting go of what does not serve you. You don't worry about naming the heaviness or identifying it. You simply intend, and intend some more, until the moment when you feel a shift: it's gone!
>
> Then you draw up lighter energy from the rich, nurturing earth, filling your cells. In this way, exchanging energy with the earth, you can explore the alchemical process of moving and shifting your own energy.

Imagine the soil, the earthworms, the water and pebbles, the seeds unfurling as you send down and draw up from the earth. In making these connections, you will be drawn out of your small self into a larger awareness, a greater integration with the world around you.

DOES THE EARTH WANT YOUR HEAVINESS?

Many people worry about giving heavy energy to the earth when they first learn about this practice. I remind them, and you, that it is just energy: the earth does not distinguish between coffee grounds, banana peels, and sadness. (Toxins and pesticides are a different story, since they affect many living beings.) Energy flows constantly throughout the universe. Whether it is heavy or light from a human perspective, it is really just energy.

WHAT DO YOU WANT TO LET GO OF?

When you are ready for a shift, change, or breakthrough, it can be really useful to name one thing you want to let go of so you can move forward. All of us have fears, and things that hold us back, and we may express this heaviness in different ways.

Look at the list of very common what-I-want-to-let-go-of experiences, and choose one you want to work with in the practice that follows:

Fear

I'm not good enough

My need to be perfect

Self-sabotage

I'm stuck

Shame

My small self-image

Holding on too tight (trying to control everything)

Perfectionism

Procrastination

My denial of who I am (anonymity)

Self-doubt

Overwhelm

I can't find a relationship

I feel alone

All of us pull in energetically like turtles when we are nervous, afraid, or sad. Inside our shells, we cannot take in or receive anything—love, compliments, appreciation, or happiness. When someone tries to give us some good energy, we may deflect it, not hear it, or dive deeper into our isolation.

If you are already a turtle in your shell, what is the worst that could happen? What do you have to lose in trying, and what might you gain?

Letting go of what keeps you separate makes an opening so you can shift, reconnect, and receive. This takes much less energy than hiding behind your shell or resisting good energy!

RELEASING AND BECOMING SOURCE

This is another simple way to practice releasing and filling. As you do it, try to visualize or feel what is happening.

> Find a word for the one thing you want to release.
>
> Breathe it out into the universe, past the stars, past blue-black space. See your word going into the heart of the universe.
>
> Breathe in the power of the universe. Breathe it into your heart. Fill your heart with the energy and power of the universe.
>
> Repeat, and keep noticing: Does your heart shift? Does your energy lift? Do you feel the power of the universe filling you?

You can release personal feelings—such as grief, fear, anger, or exhaustion. You can also release your responses to global issues—such as deforestation, animal cruelty, climate change, or violence.

Working with the Heavy Energy of Others

Working with and offering the heavy energy of other people and situations back to the earth is a practice used widely in the Peruvian Andes. It's essentially the same practice as "Eating Heavy Energy" (page 60), applied to the heaviness—drama, terror, trauma, tension, and anger—outside you. Instead of releasing your own heaviness, you are channeling the heaviness around you back into the earth.

When people around you are expressing or embodying heaviness, you can just gift it back to the earth. This moves the energy away from the human field, releases it like compost, and makes your own heart more available for compassionate witnessing.

Intent is key. As you learn to monitor your body and energy field, you get better at noticing what is not yours; you distinguish energy that is muddying the field. In an office meeting, for example, your body tension may be an internal reaction to a person or statement, or it may mirror the general tension in the room. If you are able to step back, feed the tension to the earth, and continue letting it pass through your "energetic stomach," the energy in your body and in the room will change.

In this practice, it is important to be aware of what you are "eating."

- If someone is directing heavy energy *at* you, focus on your own energetic protection and clearing. There are many practices in this book you can use to do that.

- If you feel contaminated by the energy around you, focus on releasing it from your body and energy field, and set up energetic protections. You cannot clear for others when you feel muddied yourself.

- Do not take in too much. If you experience a big sadness in your community, for example, release as much as you can to the earth, but don't exhaust yourself. Come back to working on the heaviness energetically when you can, offering the heaviness and calling in the lighter energy of love, the heavens, or the surrounding elements.

Imagine this: you are at the site of a disaster. Terror, sadness, and trauma are everywhere. If one person (you) uses this practice, the field immediately around you will feel a little better. If a hundred people, or a thousand, use this practice, how much more space might there be for everyone to take a deep breath and have a moment of spaciousness?

MOVING THE HEAVY ENERGY OF OTHERS

When you move the heaviness around you into the earth, you are not taking the energy into yourself. Instead, you visualize it flowing into an energetic channel.

Visualize an energetic channel, just beyond your belly, leading into the earth. Gather and send the heaviness around you down this channel into the earth. Draw up lighter energy from the rich, nurturing earth, frequently filling the space around you. Keep gathering, feeding, and filling. Continue this exchange of releasing and filling until the air clears or you cannot maintain your focus.

CALMING
YOUR NERVOUS SYSTEM

One of the benefits of working with energy and breath is that your physical body and nervous system can relax and calm down. In our fast-paced, distracting world, this is a gift in itself.

Every movement, meditation, and martial arts tradition teaches that the deeper your breath is, the more relaxed you are; the more relaxed you are, the more present, and the better your day goes. I have experienced this over and over again, and I'm sure you have too!

When you shift your attention from worrying or carrying heaviness in your heart to releasing the heaviness, you also release the associated tension. When you fill with lighter energy, you increase your endorphins, one of the sources of your "happy" feelings. You distract or shift your mind into a different kind of attention, perception, and presence, moving from monkey mind to a simpler, heart-based focus. You can notice this shift immediately when you stop and picture or visualize someone you love: your whole body shifts.

As you find practices that work like this for you, stick with them. Let yourself experience and enjoy the change, and do not worry about "understanding" what is going on. Remember: worry causes heavy energy!

Now that practices for pushing boulders aside and releasing energy blockages are available to you whenever you need them, it's time to explore how to fill yourself with juicy, lighter, joyful energy. In the next chapter you'll learn how to work with your three centers and will explore practices for connecting with what is always available: the earth and the natural world around you.

Chapter 4
Connecting,
Filling, and Opening

Here is the big question: what energy do you want to fill yourself with?

When you dig a hole to plant something, half the dirt automatically falls back in. Similarly, people empty their closets only to fill them back up again. Nature abhors a vacuum.

If you have released some heaviness—a problem that's been holding you back, for example—and do not intentionally fill that space with something lighter, what happens? Generally, another problem comes along to fill the hole. This is human nature: we are drawn to what is familiar, and focusing on problems and worries is what most of us do.

Yet you have a choice. You can learn to release the heavy so you can fill with the lighter, more "refined" energy. You can stop concentrating on the pain-body and focus instead on the joy-body. If you don't release your heaviness—sorrow, a bad day, resentment, and so on—you get too full to take in appreciation, or gratitude, or the joyful sight of a beautiful sunset.

Learning the pattern—release-connect-fill-open, release-connect-fill-open—helps you shift your energy, attitude, and experience.

The pattern can help you replace your cultural trance. If you habitually try to sidestep the pain-body or a heavy heart with addictions—social media, alcohol, pain pills, and so on—you have noticed that addictions mask the heaviness but do not change anything. The same unhappiness you brought home from your job is still there when you turn the TV off.

Energetically, most of us either hold in, protecting ourselves, or move through the world without boundaries. Learning the pattern—release-connect-fill-open, release-connect-fill-open—can help you shift your intent and pay more attention to what you are taking in and connecting with.

When you are able to receive and fill yourself fully with whatever is given—a hug, a compliment, an offer of help, or energy from a tree or the heart of the universe—you are able to give fully of yourself. In contrast, if you try to give without receiving and filling, you become empty, resentful, or burned out. If you only take and fill without giving back, you live from a narrow, self-centered, disconnected place. It is in the balance—of giving and receiving, emptying and filling—that your perception changes.

Moving your energy around—releasing, filling, changing stories, making connections—actually shifts feelings and fills your heart. Remember: your pain and mental responses are not *you*.

You can explore filling your body, cells, heart, and organs—your whole self—with the energy of stars or moonlight, sun or air. You can explore and build relationships with wild creatures, mountains, the black light at the center of the universe, or the magma at the center of the earth. Everything has living energy, and whatever you are drawn to is what is important for you to explore. The many practices in this book really only touch the surface of what is possible.

FILLING YOUR THREE CENTERS

Every energy system from around the world works with patterns and systems of energy flow within the body and with the outside world. Traditional Chinese medicine looks at the flow of energy through meridians; Hindu tradition focuses on the circulation of energy in the seven chakras. Andean and Celtic traditions focus on the flow and relationship between three centers.

All these energy systems are based on observation and experience—often going back thousands of years—as well as on cosmology and related belief systems. All of them focus on balance for healing. Energy wisdom traditions can be seen as kindred frameworks, says Angela Prider,

> ...used by medicine people around the world to understand, weave, and harmonize with the living energies of the cosmos that are mirrored within our beings.[1]

Throughout the book, I draw particularly on my experience with Celtic, Chinese, and Andean wisdom traditions, in which the three centers of energy in your physical body—belly, heart, and the third eye (the point above your nose between your eyebrows)—are a central focus:

- In Celtic cosmology, the three centers are known as the three cauldrons, representing your true self and your soul.
- In *qi gong*, traditional Chinese medicine, and martial arts, the three centers are known as the three *dan tien*—*xia*, *zhong*, and *shang*—focal points for meditative and exercise techniques as well as storage centers for life force energy.[2]
- In Andean cosmology, the three bands are known as the three centers of being—*llank'ay*, *munay*, and *yachay*—used for releasing heavy and taking in lighter energy.[3]

The belly, heart, and third eye centers of energy offer a simple focus for working with your energy. They are easy to remember, familiar to you already, and encoded in language: "He felt in his gut that they should hire her" or "She has a big heart." You can use them to exchange the heavy for the light; to gather your power and expand and share it; and to develop your perception, intent, and alignment.

If you know and like another system—the seven chakras, for example—you can easily use it. One of the joys of working with energy is that, once you get the hang of it, you can integrate energy practices with exercise, meditation, and your other spiritual practices, opening many doors of perception.

THE BELLY CENTER: POWER AND BEING

Your *belly* is your place of power and being. You can think of it as your wellspring: the source of wisdom gathered from your own experience, your gut instincts, and your inner fire.

In cosmic, poetic, and shamanic language, your belly is the place from which you connect your luminous fibers to others, the band from which rivers emanate, and your point of nonexistence. It is the center of your life force energy and your central connection with the field of *qi* that surrounds you. Just below the belly button, it is also known as the yogic *hara*, the Andean *qosq'o* and *waynu*, and the Chinese *dan tien (xia)*.

THE HEART CENTER: LOVE

Your *heart* is your place of love, compassion, responsiveness, and receptivity. Your heart center is activated by joy and sorrow, by love, grief, and connection: the whole range of emotions that feeds whatever you do. In heartfelt reciprocity, your interconnections flourish. Américo Yábar tells us, "The heart never chooses. Only the mind does. Our alchemy is the alchemy of heart. When the heart knows, that wisdom goes to the whole body."[4]

You can think of your heart as your receiving and transmitting device, and as the locus for unifying diverse vibrations, energies, and emotions. Your heart is the place of clear light that transforms *qi* energy into spirit. You can also think of your heart as the sound of the celestial realm (*anahata*, the fourth chakra in the yoga tradition), where masculine and feminine find union.

THE THIRD EYE CENTER: VISION

Your *third eye* center is your place of wisdom, sacred seeing, spirit, and mystery. It is filled with grace and miracles, poetry and magic, and the divine joy that feeds your vision. This center holds your energy brain. It is referred to in some traditions as the pineal gland, your "eye" of perception.

You can think of the third eye as the locus of the energy of consciousness and spirit, and as a metaphor for nondual thinking. It corresponds to the *ajna* (sixth chakra in yoga), a space behind the eyebrows, a dark or black space. In *qi gong*, this *dan tien* converts spiritual *shen* energy into *wuji*, the infinite space of the void. In the Andes, this center helps integrate wisdom and service by bringing *sami* (lighter, refined energy) into form.

LEARNING FROM YOUR THREE CENTERS

Focusing your attention on what each of your three centers communicates to you is central to becoming a warrior of the spirit: a person who acts from open heart and vision, full of power, clarity, and silence.

Your three centers are important tools for reorganizing your perception and developing your internal authority. When you move and act from the energy in your three centers, your body changes your mind; you move away from mental constructs and toward experiential engagement. Engaging all three centers and bringing them into balance is central to building resonance in your heart and experiencing your living energy universe.

Christian mystic Richard Rohr says that being aware in all three of your centers is like "having the mind of Christ." He writes,

It happens whenever, by some wondrous "coincidence," our heart space, our mind space, and our body awareness are all simultaneously open and nonresistant. I like to call it presence. It is experienced as a moment of deep inner connection, and it always pulls you, intensely satisfied, into the naked and undefended now, which can involve both profound joy and profound sadness.[5]

Becoming a "seer"—a see-er of what lies beyond the visible— means that your three centers are open: you see and perceive with your whole body, your whole energy bubble.

FILLING AND ALIGNING YOUR THREE CENTERS

Filling and aligning your three centers are central to observing and bringing them into balance. This practice helps you notice whether the centers are out of kilter, and full of energy or not. Filling and aligning help you experience what it's like when your three centers are filled up.

When you feel "out of sorts," this practice is an excellent tool for harmonizing and realigning yourself; power comes from alignment. It is a way of getting in touch with your true self, your full essence.

Place your hands on your belly, holding them just below your belly button. Visualize your belly filled with white light. See it full and spilling over with light.

Place your hands on your heart. Visualize the white light flowing upward from your belly, filling your heart and spilling over. See the light traveling back down into your belly and up again until your belly and heart feel harmonized.

Place your hands on your third eye. See the white light flowing upward from your belly and heart into your third eye. Feel your third eye full of light and spilling over, circulating down to belly and heart, and up again.

See the white light flowing between all three centers until you feel calm, full, and realigned.

Connecting, Filling, and Opening to the Earth

When you touch earth, the earth touches you. Your intent to connect paves the way.

Mother Earth, as she is called around the world, supports our feet, our cars, our homes, our water supply. You spend every day of your life with her; she's always with you! Shifting from taking her for granted to calling on her and connecting with her is simple; the energy you can draw upon to do this is profound. Indigenous peoples take in energy from the earth; you can too. What I have discovered is that the more I connect to the earth, the less alone, isolated, and disconnected I feel.

When you are tired after a long meeting, three hours of conference calls, or running around after some five-year-olds, you can use any of the following practices to release the fatigue and draw in energy from the earth, opening to her support and power. When you do this regularly, you will notice a stronger and stronger connection developing, along with a changed sense of self and ego.

GROWING YOUR ROOTS

Standing with your feet on the ground, imagine roots growing from your feet down into the soil, beyond the bedrock, all the way to the center of the earth. Draw the energy of the magma at the center up your roots, into your feet and bones, all the way up to your crown. Imagine your roots again, drawing all the fatigue and heaviness out of you, sending it into the earth. Draw up the power again. Repeat until you feel connected and refreshed.

TOUCHING EARTH

Use this practice anytime you want to shift your energy quickly.

> With your feet on the ground and your hands facing flat toward the earth, connect your energy. Feel the earth's vibrations running between your flat hands and the soil. Let yourself come into stillness in this connection. Notice how your energy shifts.

BEING EARTH

While I am walking or hiking, I like to repeat this simple phrase with each step, experiencing the reality of it in my body and my feet.

> I am earth. I am earth. I am earth. I am earth. I am earth. I am earth.

MOVING EARTH AND SKY THROUGH YOUR BODY

This very simple movement, combined with the intent to let go of whatever you were doing and shift into a state of presence, is a wonderful example of the saying, "Where your attention goes, energy flows." You might do it, for example, when you finish a phone call and walk to get a cup of tea, or when you are hiking, to remind and fill yourself with your connection to the earth and sky.

> With your palms facing down toward the earth, release any heaviness. With your palms facing up to the sky, raise your hands, pulling cosmic energy into your body and energy field. Lower your palms again, releasing any energy you need to. Raise them up again, moving energy between the earth, your body, and the cosmos. Do this for as long as you can stay focused.

LYING ON THE EARTH

Every time I suggest that my students lie belly-to-belly with the earth, there is some maneuvering as people try to get comfortable, stay clean, or avoid ants. Yet as soon as people are settled, there is an amazing shift: no one wants to get up! This simple act of connecting your umbilical cord with that of the Mother is profoundly nurturing. It is something most of us remember from childhood, even when we did not do it with much consciousness.

Lie with your belly button on the Earth. Let yourself soak in the connection, staying as long as you want. If you fall asleep, enjoy!

Experiencing, Connecting, and Opening to Nature

You have to spend time outside—observing, listening, being—to sense the environment as your extended body. Being outside with a specific tree gives you a "perceptual" or experiential sense of the feeling of its bark, leaves, and shape. Being outside offers you direct experience of the smell of wet earth, the feel of the wind, and the shifting colors of your favorite lake. The more you are outside, deeply filling yourself with such sensations, the more you become an embodied part of the whole.

Imagine you are walking through a forest. Your habit is to look at the trees and enjoy the views. Maybe you identify the birds or native plants; possibly you notice the relationships of a particular species to the environment. Maybe you can even name most plant, animal, insect, and reptile species in the ecosystem. All these skills and habits come from information about the forest; they come from the mind.

What if, noticing a bobcat, you slowly, very slowly, approach it? What if the bobcat stops and watches you? Suddenly you are paying attention to sound, movement, breath, and footfall; you are shifting out of mind. What if the bobcat lets you approach? Your heart hammers, and your body becomes very still. What if the bobcat lets you sit and share the forest, even lets you sing to him?

Now you are in your body, your senses; now you are feeling the connection with the bobcat. You have moved from *looking at* to *being with*. You've opened your resonant heart to engage with the living energy of this other being.

In this perceptual framework (heart and sensation, not mind), everything is alive and engaged in conversation. In the Quechua-Aymara world, this reciprocal interaction is described as follows:

The Andean does not experience gazing at the rising of a constellation in a particular region on the horizon as a unidirectional act ... Rather it is experienced as the constellation and gazer being united in a conversation."[6]

Our perception is central. When I was separated from my former husband and considering divorce, I lived at the edge of open-space woodlands. In my deep sorrow and loss, I was drawn to an ancient oak tree near my cabin—an oak ten times my age, a being who had seen far more of the world than I had. I found solace in being reminded of my smallness in the scheme of things; it was as if my heartbreak lessened as I engaged with this oak every day. A long time before I knew that other people acknowledged and depended on such interaction, I was gifted with this "conversation" that helped me survive.

DEEPENING YOUR RELATIONSHIP WITH ONE PLACE

Establishing a relationship with the natural world is like nurturing one with a human: it takes care, time, intent, and mutual exchange.

I read about a man in Arizona who took the same hike in the mountains around Tucson every day for ten years. His deep familiarity let him know the seasons, the effects of drought on the creatures and plants, and changes over time. Many cultures have practices like this: a Zen Buddhist monk is assigned a nine-year, daily cycle of circumambulation; a young Masai warrior is instructed, as part of his initiation, to go into the bush with nothing but his spear until he kills a lion. Luckily, lion killing is not part of our culture, and there are other ways to practice deepening by establishing your relationship with place.

Return to one place—a single tree, a lake, a stream, a mountain, a trail near where you live, a corner of the park—regularly. Experience it with all your senses—feel the breeze on your face, taste the warmth of the sun on your skin, let the sounds vibrate into your cells, and notice when the energy changes. The more you know it, the more you deepen and expand your awareness of who lives there, how the seasons change, what plant beings thrive there. With this understanding, your perception grows and grows, as does your connection. Out of connection flows reciprocity.

OBSERVING YOUR GARDEN

Your grandparents or great-grandparents probably had a "victory garden" during World War II: because many staples were not available, and to help the country fight the war, this was common. So not very long ago your own relatives knew gardening or farming, and you can learn these skills again. If you want a practical way to reconnect with the earth, seasonal cycles, and your food sources, you don't need to leave your gardening to others.

Start with one plant. Make a relationship with it by preparing the soil, weeding and watering and nurturing it, harvesting and being nurtured by its fruits.

Learn where and how each of your plants thrives: what soil, terroir, water, nutrients, and creatures help them grow? How do the seasons and droughts affect various plants? Can you observe enough to discover how they survive natural challenges?

Talk to the farmers at your local farmer's market to learn more, and visit their farms if you can.

DRINKING MOONLIGHT

This practice is based on the baby unicorns who drink moonlight for their sustenance in Madeline L'Engle's children's book *A Wrinkle in Time*. You can too!

Facing the moon, tip your head back and open your mouth so moonlight hits the roof of your mouth. Swallow the moonlight, drinking it in. Feel and see the bright moonlight spreading through your whole torso and into all your cells.

CLEANSING AND FILLING WITH WIND

Wind has power to bring storms, move pollution, and carry burning heat and cooling fog. You draw on this power in your body daily. Consciously engaging with cleansing air gives you a tool that's always accessible for releasing and filling. Just as your exercise teachers remind you, "Breathe deeply!"

> Lie on your back, legs stretched out, with your arms at your sides. Breathe fresh air up through your feet, legs, torso, and out your crown.
>
> Release all the stale air, starting at your head and breathing down to your feet and out. Breathe in again, letting the freshness fill every cell and organ. Breathe out again, intending to release all toxins and discomfort.
>
> Repeat until your body feels calm and refreshed.

ENGAGING WITH WATER

While you probably do it automatically—think of kids' glee as they race toward a lake or ocean—you can engage more consciously with any body of water. You can reconnect with your fluidity beside rivers and streams. You can feed your natural rhythms with the soothing movement of ocean waves. You can deepen your connection with water in very wet climates by noticing that it is no different outside (80 percent humidity) than it is inside (our bodies are 70 to 80 percent water).

> Facing the water, feel its flow in your own blood. As you touch the water with your hands or feet or whole body, let your organs and cells take in the constant movement, the sense of washing over, and the fluidity.
>
> Reflecting on the cycle of each drop—from stream to river to ocean, from ocean evaporating into air, from air into fog or rain cloud or snow, drifting back down to earth to begin the cycle again—imagine how you can mirror that kind of spiraling connection in your life.

SPONTANEOUS FILLING AND CONNECTING WITH THE ELEMENTS

Since the elements surround and live within you, they offer many possibilities for spontaneous filling, connecting, opening, and shifting. Here are some options:

> Lie on the earth. Let your whole body slow to match the earth's rhythm, breathing in resonance.
>
> Study the morning sunlight on the dew. Revel in the reflecting rainbow colors to remind yourself of your beautiful light essence.
>
> When a sudden gust of wind blows, release!
>
> Offer your heavy energy to water every time you pee.
>
> Take a short walk, paying full attention to each step. Notice the roots coming out of your feet into the ground, the air caressing you, the sun filling you with light.
>
> Walk, concentrating on one element for five minutes. Say "water, water, water" with each step to stay focused on water. Pay attention to the water in your body. Then say "air, air, air" to focus on air (and so on).

Now that you are releasing, connecting, filling, and opening to the living energy around you—the elements, nature, and earth herself—I invite you to investigate another essential part of the process. Exploring the stories you tell, and shifting your focus and perception of events, are the next steps in Energy Alchemy.

Chapter 5
Changing Your
Challenging Stories

The stories you tell can be funny, destructive, affirming, and everything in between. You might tell a story to entertain, to establish your identity, to teach a lesson, or to fill a lull in the conversation. You might tell a story to convince, to get attention, to brag, to make sense of a difficult situation, or to hear yourself talk. Very few people tell mean stories intentionally; rather, they are unconscious of the effects of what they say, or are so self-involved they don't notice.

For most of human history, stories were enlightening reminders of how to live. In modern culture, children's stories come closest to the old intentions, offering imaginative, zany, and wise advice.

Our cultural and national stories often represent collective belief, or what those in power want us to believe: who the "enemy" is, why we need to destroy certain tribes, peoples, or nations; how "reality" justifies our actions. Such stories carry the power of ideology.

Similarly, the stories we use to make sense of a personal situation also act as justifications. Think of your friends who say, "My ex-husband was a jerk," "My ex-wife ripped me off in the divorce settlement," or "I have a bad back so I can't work/help you move/take care of the kids." In the context of working with challenging stories, these kinds—especially those we repeat again and again—are, essentially, internal dialogue that we use to create the reality we believe in.

Stories are constructed from both words and energy—the emotions behind the words. So changing your challenging stories has two aspects. The first is to reflect on the words you use and your intent in telling a story. The second is to release any energy—whether anger, embarrassment, shame, or even despair—associated with the story.

DEFINING "REALITY" WITH STORIES

It's common in Western culture to think about *why* we feel a certain way. We often tell stories that assign blame—naming who or what caused our feelings. When we repeat these stories, we give them more energy by revisualizing and recreating the wrong done to us. Energetically, we are creating density and heaviness by feeding the negative. Once the story defines our reality, we are more likely to expect the story to continue; we are more likely to step into another, parallel situation.

As we recreate the feelings we had with storytelling, those feelings become our reality, and they may become reality for others in the story too: the family "black sheep" lives as we expect him to; the "terrorist" keeps acting like one. We see this in our personal lives, families, communities, and nations.

Culturally it is easier—whether we are an individual or a president—to get attention when we have a crisis or problem. The world is addicted to bad news.

Because the stories we tell ourselves—our perceptions of experience—remain in our unconscious, they continue to influence how we perceive events in the here and now. So how do we change that? What stories do we to tell? What intent do we feed?

REFRAMING NEGATIVE SELF-TALK TO SHIFT YOUR STORY

You bind up everything you experience—energy, emotions, traumas—with your thoughts, stories, and beliefs. When you have lived with a negative feeling or story about yourself all your life, it may be hidden or unconscious, or it may be so familiar you don't notice it.

Reframing—or unbinding—such a story happens gradually. It begins with bringing the story to awareness. After that, it takes patience, perseverance, and strong intent. The process moves you away from rigidity and toward flow and ease.

One of my clients, the "black sheep" in his family, was recovering from a divorce and had just started a new job. He had found a place to live near his job, and wanted to move there, yet his friends lived in another city.

His negative self-talk came out gradually. I listened as he berated himself about the job: "I was sick and didn't negotiate for myself. I didn't ask for as much money as I should have." To help him reframe both story and outcome, I taught him to release and fill, and suggested he keep a list of his accomplishments. We practiced how he might go back to his employer and renegotiate—and he succeeded.

Next time we talked he was unhappy about his relationships: friends far away, no success in finding people he liked, no good women out there. As he told me all of this, he became increasingly upset. His siblings' mean treatment of him—more loyal to his ex-wife than to their own brother—came out. In a half hour, he had gone from being focused on change to a despairing, weeping muddle of self-loathing. Woven into his present circumstances were past treatment, perceived experience, and a life story of not being enough.

"What happens to us is not as important as our experience of it," as psychologist Stanley Krippner says.[1] Awareness and change begin when someone—therapist, friend, healer—helps you see *the difference between a problem in the present and your lifelong assumptions*. Once you are aware of the disconnection between your experience and the situation, your challenge is to learn to notice and identify your gut response, then shift your perception and energetic response. Then you practice shifting, and you repeat that practice. Watching the energy, listening to the words, paying attention to somatic messages, and learning *how* you respond are all ways of facilitating this shift.

I have a lifelong experience of perceiving myself as not good enough. Despite many successes, I *felt* not enough. Therapy didn't help. I didn't understand that it was my perception—applying my deeply held assumptions (actually, my parents' deeply held assumptions passed on to me)—not "reality." It took listening to voice recordings of myself telling the same not-enough story repeatedly, along with someone else's clarity about my root response, to clue me in.

Since I was really tired of the story's effects in my life, I had a strong intent to figure out a different way to respond. Even then, it took hard work and perseverance. At first, it took at least a week after a triggering event for my pattern to dawn on me, and, once it entered my awareness, I followed up with what felt like endless linear pro-cessing and self-talk to shift my perception. Gradually I got faster at identifying my pattern: in a few days, then in one day, then in an hour I could figure out what was going on. I learned that the pattern never fully disappears, but you can manage it, shift your perception, and change your response.

When I learned to release heavy energy and fill with something lighter, change became less cumbersome. Instead of endless analysis, I could work with my energy to shift my experience of and engagement with the world. If I had known about energetic releasing and filling thirty years ago, life would have been easier!

REFRAMING TRAUMA
TO SHIFT YOUR STORY

All of us store trauma-induced emotions in our bodies. They may man-ifest as physical or spiritual illness. They are rarely responsive to mental understanding. Discovering and working with the energy behind your traumatic emotions are powerful ways to help mitigate the damage and shift your responses.

It is your limbic (reptilian) brain that triggers your animal-like, fight-or-flight responses to abuse, rape, prolonged violence, warfare, or accidents, including those your ancestors experienced. This part of your brain *does not respond to words at all*. Traumatic experiences and their associated emotions are essentially walled off from conceptual understanding. More and more research tells us that to stop the night-mares and stop reenacting the trauma in our families, workplaces, and nations, we have to replace the traumatic experiences, heal the soul, and essentially create a different identity.[2]

I know a number of veterans who have successfully shifted identi-ties and healed in this way over the course of many years. Shifting from a warrior stance into a deeply different focus of energy and attention—becoming, variously, poet, passionate activist for change, therapist, and online bookseller—they were able to move their thoughts and dreams away from post-traumatic stress and toward gentler ways of being.

No matter what experiences and emotions you have, when you want to widen, change, and open your perceptions, you have to consciously push the boulders aside and release whatever stands in the way. Then you have to be willing to try new things and fill yourself with different experiences.

The key to changing your perception is releasing what no longer serves you—the old and heavy energy—and replacing it with new, lighter, more appropriate experiences. You could also think of this as unlearning and relearning. It helps to reflect on and formulate your intent. It helps to try to experience as a child does, with "fresh eyes," without the barriers of ideas, rules, and filters between mind and heart. The shifting of perception follows experience.

Working with Story Shape

Stories you tell about your children (or that were told about you) are a great example of how to work with and reshape stories. The story that follows is based on a real situation, although I have changed names, specifics, and the outcome.

The parents in a certain family had strong moral values and puritanical tendencies. One son was born under difficult circumstances, was quite ill as a young child, and was perceived as "difficult." Many of his behaviors were confusing, challenging, and befuddling to the parents. In high school, the son received multiple mental illness diagnoses; his previous behaviors began to make sense in this context. Relieved after years of stress, the parents began repeating his diagnosis and telling this story: "He is challenged. He is ill." Finally they had some "answers."

Their original intent (an unconscious one) was to "make sense" of the situation. After a while, they told the story of the son's mental illness as a way to get sympathy and attention: "This is what we've been going through," and so on. From the parents' perspective, there was a real need for this story. As the son's story became embedded in the family's story, a "reality" was created: everyone's experience (son, parents, siblings, family friends, and teachers) was molded and affected by the story.

When the son left home, he carried the heavy burden of his story. He made many attempts to overcome it, but the parents' story continued unchanged.

Then an extended family drama unfolded. The story led to incorrect assumptions, misunderstandings, cruel accusations, and a huge upset within the family. The son was hurt, more misunderstandings ensued, and a lot of energy was spent smoothing things over.

For the parents, this was a wake-up call, an opportunity to consciously reflect on their intent. They asked, "Why are we telling this story? It doesn't serve our son, it doesn't serve us, and it obviously led to false assumptions. *Now* what story are we going to tell, if any?"

Finding a new story was not easy for these parents. But with a different intent—to support their adult son in his quest for wholeness, whatever that would mean to him, and to let go of their habit of taking his behavior personally—they began to explore a new story. There were fits and starts; they tried out different responses. Finally it became clear that a simple, lighter, son-affirming response would be best. They wanted to avoid adding any heavy energy to their son's path; their intent was to be positive or neutral. When people asked about him, they replied, "He's doing great." If they had a specific, positive anecdote they would add one. If not, they made a general statement about what their son was up to.

The energetic effects of this were very interesting. The parents were able to experience their son's life and challenges as *his* (rather than theirs to fix or apologize for). The son felt freer to be who he was, no excuses. All of them were able to enjoy each other more. The story had become a heavy boulder, and removing it made the way for lighter energy in all aspects of the family's dynamics. Changing the story changed everyone's perceptions.

SHIFTING PERCEPTION WITH DREAM STORY

Your dreams often replay and recreate your experiences and perceptions, repeating your internal dialogue. One of my teachers, the healer Mandaza Kandemwa from Zimbabwe, had advised me to keep asking for "clear sleeping dreams and visions, messages that do not need interpretation." Shortly afterward, my dreams themselves began to shift my perceptions by showing me my old stories, and then transforming them.

In my dream I am on a group trip. Scenes that remind me of many old failures pass before my eyes: the cute guy goes for someone else. I am slow to get the picture. I bog down in my "luggage" of stones and books. I am not a leader, not one of the "important" ones. I don't shine the way I could. I find the people boring, disconnected, and disappointing.

The trip ends; people disperse. Then the group members begin to return, connecting with each other and having fun. I join them at long tables. Suddenly it is an animated, engaged time. I watch the jewels in all these ordinary (and formerly "boring") people come out. I am amazed.

This dream was a gift, changing "boring" people into "jewels" and *showing me I could experience life differently.* It drew on the more hopeful and appreciative framework I inhabit now, helping me release my old perceptions.

The same gift is possible for you as you "dream a new dream" for yourself, your family, and our world.

SHIFTING YOUR FOCUS

I used to believe it was okay to swear at the driver who cut me off, or get irritated with the customer service representative who wouldn't or couldn't fix my problem. Does this sound familiar?

Then I learned about the effects of energy. I came to understand that the energy behind my words was going out into the world whether or not the person could hear me. I also noticed that when I expressed irritation, I was more likely to remain irritated, creating heavy energy for myself and anyone around me. By feeding my story, however "minor" in the scheme of things, I was feeding a certain reality.

I spent a lot of years learning to shift my focus, and to stop putting blaming energy into the world. This is not easy in a culture where the media, politicians, and our friends blame others out of habit, and fan the fires of anger and retribution.

One of my clients, Virginia, described how shifting her focus changed her life:

I've been working with the intent to release heaviness—instead of holding on to it, repeating it, telling poor-me stories about it—for a long time. I let go of cranky thoughts a lot faster, so I enjoy my life more. I spend much less time and energy suffering over presumed insults, upsets, and the 'negative' things that happen. I have more energy for creativity and compassion. I am able to focus less on the personal and more on the communal.

QUICK SHIFTING-FOCUS PRACTICES

These are a few of the practices you can use to shift your focus:

- Open the crown of your head. Let light flow into you, filling your body, cells, and heart. Notice that concentrating on the light shifts your focus away from irritation.

- Remind yourself that the other is not the problem.

- Instead of running an old tape that upsets you, visualize the face of someone or something you love. Feel your heart fill with the good energy of that relationship.

- Practice forgiveness: remind yourself that the crazy driver, surly teenager, or bored salesperson is probably having a bad day and could use some good energy from you.

- Choose a different visual image—a sunset, a happy baby, your best friend laughing— for each day of the week. Find and print out these images, or just keep a list. When you feel your energy getting heavy or your stories turning negative, call up the image of the day, shifting your focus to shift your energy.

QUESTIONS TO ASK

By studying your stories' shapes, you can change them and spin them into power.

As you work on moving your boulders, focus on becoming more attentive. Notice how things feel after you tell a story. Notice the energy in your body and the energy in the room. When you notice heavy effects in your three centers, in the room, or in the person the story concerns, ask:

- What am I feeding by telling this story? Does it help me look better? Get sympathy? Be right while the other person is wrong?
- Am I hiding a secret by telling this story? (Secrets lead to stress, according to neuroscientists.)
- What focus, framework, and "lesson" would serve my intent better?
- How can I honor the past and the lessons I have learned without feeding the old hurts and picking the scab?

As you ask these questions, keep releasing the energy that arises. Fill yourself with lighter, more joyful energy or a nurturing image like the face of someone you love.

DIS-CREATION VISUALIZATION

Our beliefs are at the root of our stories and fuel them. When you identify a belief that no longer serves you and that you no longer want, here is a fun and easy way to release the energy of that belief. Analysis may work, but it often gets us stuck in our mental constructs. "Dis-creating" the belief often works better.

Children like releasing their fears this way. (And they are usually better than adults at naming the feeling behind the belief.)

DIS-CREATING A BELIEF

Working with strong intent to release a belief will help you let go more easily.

Choose a belief you want to dis-create. Feel it—experience it in your body. Give the feeling a name.

See the name inside a bubble. Watch the bubble float up, up into the sky and away from you. Watch it go as far as you are able into the sky. When you can barely see it, pop the bubble with a pin. You can say, "This is not me: this is my creation" if you want.

Repeat: Watch the bubble float away. Pop the bubble when you can barely see it. Repeat again and again until you can't feel the belief inside you anymore. You will feel the shift in your body as the thought loses its energy and power. Celebrate the spaciousness in your body!

If you are ambivalent about letting a belief go, or it is a deeply held one, you may find yourself popping the bubble again and again. Keep trying: if you have had this belief for a long time, it may take more than a few dis-creations to loosen and release it.

Practicing Forgiveness: Ho'opono'pono

When there is a misunderstanding or when you find yourself carrying a grudge, speaking the simple words from an ancient Hawaiian practice, *Ho'opono'pono,* can be healing. When you try them out aloud, you will see how profound they are: you can *feel* your residual resistance in your body and heart.

Ho'opono'pono is powerful because the emotions of gratitude and forgiveness hold great alchemical power. It is powerful because we are not really separate; we are all part of each other.

There are many, and more complex, versions of *Ho'opono'pono.* I like this one because I can remember the words and it gets right to the point. You can say this directly to someone or something (the earth, or a creature you have inadvertently killed). You can also put the energy of your words into the universe, speaking to someone from your heart.

USING HO'OPONO'PONO FOR FORGIVENESS

Say:
I am sorry. Please forgive me. I love you.
I am sorry. Please forgive me. I love you.
I am sorry. Please forgive me. I love you.

Notice how things shift in your body.

Attending to Your Judging Mind

No matter where you are in your life—no matter how spiritual, aware, and conscious you are—you will get pulled into judgment of yourself and others.

Yet judgment isn't really useful. It keeps you stuck in negative self-talk, I-am-better-than-he-is thoughts, and competition. Judgment comes from your mind, not your heart.

Your judgments keep you from believing in new possibilities. Personal affirmations often don't work because your hidden judgments sabotage them. Dreaming a new story into being can be problematic if those hidden judgments lead you to believe something is impossible. Finding the perfect mate? Talking to spirits? Creating new energetic structures? Changing the energy in your cells? Developing new DNA?

We all hold ourselves back, and protect ourselves from having to change, by grasping, feeding, and holding on to our judgments.

You have about eighty-five thousand thoughts each day. How many of them feed your judgments, stories, and habits? As Cynthia Sue Larson explains,

> ... the average person hears between 300 and 1,000 words of self-talk each and every minute—so learning to quiet or improve the quality of all this inner chatter can make a big difference in our lives ... taking a few minutes a day to meditate and silence inner chatter helps to develop a wonderful quality of inner peacefulness by which new information and experiences have room to arrive. And the more you meditate, the more likely you are to notice your self-talk becoming increasingly more positive.[3]

SHIFTING YOUR JUDGMENTS

This simple practice for shifting your judgments and perceptions has profound effects, especially if spoken aloud. When you find yourself making a judgment of any kind, you can consciously add "so am I" to your thought. I like balancing both negative and positive judgments this way.

It works like this:

He is so stupid—so am I.
She is so stubborn—so am I.
She is so ignorant—so am I.
He is such a jerk—so am I.
They are so beautiful—so am I.
They are so wise—so am I.
They are just the way they are—so am I.
She is so loving—so am I.

Now that I have shown you some ways to explore shifting focus, perceiving differently, practicing forgiveness, and shifting your judgments, I invite you to delve deeper into moving and shifting your energy. The next chapter will help you develop skill in exchanging energy with the elements, moving energy with your heart, and being in relationship with the living beings around you.

Chapter 6
Finding Fluidity:
Moving Your Energy

When you live in relationship with everything around you, it is natural to move with fluidity, responding to mood, weather, animals and plants, the challenges and joys of your community. When you spend your life indoors—at desks or computers, checking your mobile devices all day—it is more natural to move distractedly from one thing to the next. Most of us live static, atomized, and repetitive lives. Both children and adults look *at* something all day long, rather than playing, hanging out, just being.

When my teachers in the Andes talked about fluidity, I was so stuck in my repetitive life habits that I literally didn't understand what they were talking about. One day, after a long and beautiful ceremony beside a lake, I saw fluidity in action. Our Q'ero companions stepped from one world—that of ceremony and connection to the energies of the cosmos—into another, one of commerce and livelihood, in seconds. Now they were ready to sell their gorgeous weavings, a major source of cash in a subsistence economy, while we Western visitors continued to wander around blissful and spaced out, unable to bargain or even think about cost.

Now I think of fluidity as being like a river: like water, I move slowly or rapidly, get caught in eddies, stagnate, find still pools, and am always aware of my energetic movement. Even when I am feeling great emotional discomfort, I do the practices that I know will help me shift and move my energy to a different state.

To help you enhance your sense of fluidity, this chapter builds on the energy exchange, connection, and movement practices you have already learned. It guides you in shifting from the mental and emotional—anger, depression, or despair at the state of the world—into somatic experience. It helps you draw on your intuition and sensation as you work in relationship with something beyond yourself, such as the elements. As you engage inside with outside—just as when you breathe out and breathe in air—you become interpenetrated with other living energies. You fill yourself with energy that is more appropriate to and supportive of who you are: energy that feeds your heart rather than weighing it down.

Energy Exchange

Making a practice of energy exchange—releasing and filling, releasing and filling—is central to transformation. Paying attention to moving your energy helps you learn fluidity.

When movement stops, energy stagnates.

The basic principle of energy exchange—that whenever you release something heavy, it is important to fill yourself with lighter, more refined energy—helps protect you from filling up the space you have emptied with density, negativity, or problems. You learn energetic fluidity—moving from pain-body to joy-body—as you embody the process. You make your life easier as you teach yourself the habit of releasing and filling. This takes intent, action, focus, and practice.

Energy exchange is an essential aid in replacing just about any thought pattern, story, or habit. When you release impediments to change and take in something lighter, you create spaciousness. In that spaciousness lies the possibility for new thought patterns, stories, and experiences. Energy exchange is a way of developing energetic solutions to the problems you face.

You can exchange energy with any other living being: a plant in your office, a mountain, a boulder you are climbing, an animal you love, a weed in the sidewalk. You may be surprised at the power of this practice; I was. On one of my early visits to the Andes, after a healing, I wrapped myself in my poncho and lay in the garden watching the brilliant stars. I was filled with their vastness, quietude, and depth. When I exchanged energy with the great mother eucalyptus tree nearby, I traveled to the stars.

I float in the silence of the universe; plants float with me in the still blackness between the stars. The universe sparkles, darkness illuminated by star bodies, my heart opening to all.

EXCHANGING ENERGY WITH A TREE

Trees are sweet beings to exchange energy with. In this practice, instead of working with heavy and light energy, you are simply trading energy with the tree. You can think of it as a practice of complementarity, each of you sharing what you have that the other needs.

Because trees are quite sensitive, it is important to do this exchange fairly quickly. The tree will never take "too much," and you will know in your body when it is time to stop.

> Ask permission to exchange energy with a tree you like. Stand with your back against the tree, arms open, hands touching the bark. Let your energetic body and your awareness open. Receive, passively and through all your senses, whatever the tree offers you. This may be insight, a feeling, an understanding, a sensation, or a nourishing moment of stillness.
>
> Now trade roles, allowing the tree to receive whatever it needs from you energetically. Simply be there, open. Experience the resonance between you and tree.

We humans are quite oriented toward actively *giving* and *receiving*, so the opportunity to simply be present without effort and experience the exchange is both challenge and gift. You can try this same practice back-to-back with another person as well.

Deepening Your Elemental Connections Through Meditation

Your body is made up of the physical elements—minerals (earth), water, fire, and air—so your potential for connection with them is deep and profound. As Tenzin Wangyal Rinpoche writes, "The elements are all that exist, so we can always do practice with the elements, at any time, wherever we are, whatever we are doing."[1]

The elements have been on the earth in some form since the beginning. They link you to past and future, across space and time. The air you breathe also passed through the bodies of dinosaurs and Genghis Khan, and the water you drink has passed through ocean and glacier, ice age and warming—both have been present since the earth was formed.

Like us, the elements change.

When you attune, fill, align with, and find yourself in resonance with the elements, you become more than the sum of the parts. You automatically step into an expanded, connected state, where personal stories, to-do lists, and monkey mind fade. Your energy shifts and moves into a sense of floating union. Notice how empowering it is to experience such connection.

THE ELEMENTS MEDITATION

This meditation is an expanded version of what you learned in chapter 2 (releasing and filling with the elements). I love combining the elements in this way, as it helps me experience their differences. And it has a cumulative effect; when you practice the meditation regularly, your energy will automatically release, shift, and reconnect.

This is a wonderful practice for strengthening your intent and skills in releasing heavy thoughts, beliefs, and experiences and replacing them with the light, refined energy of the four elements.

The meditation also deepens your understanding of and connection to the elements, inside and out. It is a powerful tool for lightening the world and teaching yourself fluidity.[2]

Open the top of your aura, your energy bubble, and receive refined light energy from the cosmos, the Upper World, the Divine.

Let any heavy energy in you drain through your body, down your legs, and out through your feet.

Open the center at the base of your spine, at your tailbone, and visualize a pathway to the nearest water: a river, a lake, the ocean, or the aquifer beneath you. Release any heavy energy in you to the water as a gift.

Now breathe the wonderful fluid energy of water up into your tail center. Let it join with all the water in your body. Repeat this until you feel full of fresh, clear running water.

Open the center in your belly and visualize a pathway from your belly into the earth. Send any heavy energy in you to the earth as a gift.

Now breathe earth energy into your belly. Let it flow to all the organs of your body, to your bones, your cells, your skin. Repeat this until you feel full.

Open your heart to the sun. Visualize a pathway from your heart to the sun. Release any heavy energy in you to the sun, our star, as a gift.

Now breathe light, refined energy from the sun into your heart. Let your heart warm and glow. Feel the glow spread out through all the blood vessels and cells of your body. Repeat this until you feel full.

Open your throat center to the wind, moon, and stars. Let any heavy energy in you flow out through your throat on the wind to the moon and the stars, as a gift.

Now breathe in the refined energy of the wind, the moon, and the stars through your throat center. Let their light fill your brain, flow down your spine, and spread through your nervous system. Repeat this until you feel full.

Keeping these four centers—base of the spine, belly, heart, and throat—open to water, earth, sun, and wind, open the top of your energy bubble again, as you did in the beginning, to receive the refined energy of the Divine. Feel it flowing freely to balance and harmonize all the energies in your body.

Feel all the light, refined energies of water, earth, sun, air, and the Divine fill you completely, lighting your cells, your blood, your tissue, your organs, your muscles and your whole energy field.

Notice your focus, thoughts, and heart. Has worry dissipated? Do you have fresh energy, the ability to take a new look?

CREATING SACRED SPACE WITH THE ELEMENTS MEDITATION

When you create sacred space for yourself, for a ceremony, or for a group—greeting the four directions and the center with rattling or drumming—it is easy to incorporate the Elements Meditation.

It is a great way to help a group shift energy into focus and presence: when you encourage and guide people in releasing any heavy thoughts, energy, and stories they came with, and taking in the lighter energy of the elements, they are better able to experience what you are all doing together.

Incorporating the rhythms and vibrations of percussion instruments shifts your brain waves into a meditative (theta) state. Essentially, this helps drown out or distract your mind from thoughts that keep you from being present.

Try it yourself:

> As you rattle or drum in each direction, breathe out into the relevant element and draw its energy back into your body. Visualize the qualities of each element, letting your intuition guide you in what you specifically need to fill with.

For example, in the tradition I follow, wind is associated with east, fire and the sun with south, water with west, and earth with north. So as I face east, I open my throat to the wind, moon, and stars, breathing out any heaviness, and breathing in the cleansing energy of the wind. As I face south, I open my heart to the sun, breathing out any heaviness, and breathing in the transforming energy of fire. And so on.

Some indigenous traditions associate the elements with different directions than I use. If your practice is different from mine, you can modify the meditation accordingly.

PRACTICES FOR MOVING YOUR ENERGY

Most indigenous people around the world use music, dance, and trance to move their energy and reconnect. This example, from the San Bushmen, is particularly inspiring.

> *When a San Bushman community in southern Africa begins to feel disconnected, they hold a trance dance. Everyone dances till they drop, literally (this may take 24 hours). Meanwhile, the village shaman removes the stuff—feelings, old grudges, mis-communications—that's*

creating disharmony. "In the morning we all love each other again,"
the Bushmen say.[3]

SENSORY RECAPITULATION BEFORE SLEEP

Just prior to sleep is a good time to let go of the stuff of your day. The
more you cleanse, the less heaviness you carry.

Five minutes before you sleep, track back through your day, seeing and feeling any stuck places, uncomfortable moments, or what
feel like blockages.

Release them, forgive yourself, and keep moving. Don't let your
mind get stuck on an event or the story surrounding it.

Ask for clarifying dreams. If you can't clear something, put it aside
until later. See yourself radiant with light before you sleep.

FIRE BREATHING

This very simple yoga fire breath is a fast, easy way to release tension
(heaviness) and gather energy.[4] I used to do this in the car on the
way from work to pick up my daughter. It helped me shift my brain
away from the energy of business and artificial deadlines and into the
receptive energy of being with a child.

Breathe through your nose with mouth closed. Breathe in, then
out, deeply, through your belly. Take in a second deep breath into
your belly and blow out and in more and more quickly, as if you are
breathing fire like a dragon. Continue breathing very fast through
your nose until you run out of breath. Take another deep breath
in, and repeat. Do four rounds of fire breathing. Notice your heart,
your mind, and your energy field when you have finished.

TONING

Toning uses breath, voice, tongue, and interior of the mouth to elon-
gate a sound, note, tone, or syllable. It is a way to play with vibrations,
exploring them in your body and energy field and discovering how
they make you feel. Toning in a group helps the group maintain focus
on, for example, maintaining an openhearted state. The English vowel
sounds—A, E, I, O, U—are easy to use in toning.

To tone, stand or sit with your back straight. Take a deep breath and, from your belly, let the sound rise up and out until you run out of breath. Repeat, and let the tone become louder. Repeat again. Then try a different vowel.

SHAKING YOUR ENERGY BODY TO RELEASE

Twelve hours after a major earthquake, which rocked our home for several minutes yet broke only one pot, I still felt a cognitive dissonance: how could we have emerged so intact when the shaking had been so strong? A friend suggested I shake out everything that didn't belong. Following her advice, I stood near the doorway where I'd held on for dear life twelve hours earlier, and let myself shake. My body mirrored the quake immediately, shaking just as before: sharp jolts, then rocking and rolling until I came to a standstill. I was so surprised that I did it again, and realized I was releasing the trauma by re-experiencing the event.

Around the world this is loosely referred to as shaking medicine. As Bradford Keeney writes,

Shaking is the key to a wild place, the unconscious wilderness—a place that the poet Gary Snyder describes as "elegantly self-disciplined, self-regulating"—a place without a management plan. This place of wilderness is home to the shamans, Quakers, Gnostics, Taoists, yoginis, anarchists, American Indians, alchemists, Bushmen, Shakers, Sufis, Teilhard de Chardin Catholics, biologists, Druids, Zen Buddhists, and Tibetans—traditions awed by mysteries that are greater than our capacity to understand.[5]

It's not necessary to save shaking for trauma: you can use it anytime to release and move whatever energy does not serve you. It's also quite fun to do in groups.

With your feet planted, let the shaking begin in your legs, and rise up through your torso, arms, and whole body. Raise your arms above your head while you shake, and then lower them. Let the movement take over your body in whatever way it needs to, intending to let it all go. Shake until you naturally slow down and stop. Notice whatever arises in your awareness.

SPINNING YOUR CHAKRAS
TO RELEASE AND BALANCE THEM

In Hindu and Buddhist traditions, the chakras define energy centers in the body, each of which is connected to major organs and glands. Chakras, often seen as swirling disks or vortexes of energy, are used for collecting, moving, and releasing energy.

While there is no standard system in ancient texts, Westerners normally refer to seven chakras, perceived as the seven colors of the rainbow. Each color has an associated vibration and frequency. The first, at the base of your spine, is associated with the color red; the second, at your sacrum, with the color orange; the third, at your solar plexus, with the color yellow; the fourth, at your heart, with the color green; the fifth, at your throat, with the color blue; the sixth, at your third eye/brow, with the color indigo, and the seventh, at your crown, with the color white.

In the Andean tradition, spirit's rainbow body (k'uychi) is said to come down, reaching out to us and swirling in our energy field. An eighth chakra resides at the top of our aura or luminous energy field; a ninth represents the cosmos, extending through the vastness of space.[6] Chakras are spun counterclockwise to remove density and sludge, and clockwise to balance their spin and vibration.

Visualizing the chakras spinning and in color as you rotate the flat of your hand in a circle—parallel to your body—helps you embody this practice. Many people like to do it in the shower.[7]

Open your first chakra (red) with a counterclockwise hand movement a few inches above the skin (imagine your body as the face of a clock). Release and rinse any "sludge" from your fingers.

Open your other chakras in the same way. Repeat the counterclockwise spinning hand movement with the second chakra (orange), the third chakra (yellow), the fourth chakra (green), the fifth chakra (blue), the sixth chakra (indigo), and the seventh chakra (white). Release and rinse sludge from your fingers after each chakra.

Now close your chakras, beginning with the seventh and moving down to the first, with clockwise hand movements to optimize their spinning frequency.

ENTRAINING YOUR RHYTHMS WITH THE MOON

The moon is present every night of your life, cycling between waxing, full, waning, and dark (absent from view). The more you attune with the moon, the more you can move your energy, entraining your body and intent with its cycles.

Engaging with the moon's rhythms helps remind you of your own life's rhythms, and your own inner light. It also connects you to the night sky and one of our planet's beautiful allies, making your sense of the world bigger. It is one of my favorite ways of setting my intent for aligning, releasing and filling.

The first step is to notice the moon's rhythms. The second is to connect your intent with these rhythms. When it is waxing, intend to grow something in your life. When it is full, intend to connect with others. When it is waning, intend to release and let go of a particular energy. When the moon is dark, rest in your potential.

After a while of doing this, your body will draw you outside, almost of its own volition, to help you come into resonance with moon.

When the moon is waxing (for about two weeks, from new moon to full), go outside and connect your belly, heart, and third eye with the growing moon. Set your intent that something you are growing in your life (a project, an idea, a baby) draws power from the moonlight's growth. Use the growing moon to remind yourself each night of what you are growing.

When the moon is full, swallow its light. Feed the web of light with your radiance (see "Weaving a Web of Light at the Full Moon" (page 163)).

When the moon is waning (for about two weeks, from full to dark), go outside and connect with the moon. Set your intent to release something you are ready to let go of. Use the diminishing moonlight each night to remind yourself of what you are releasing.

When the moon is dark (three nights), let yourself rest in the potential that abides in darkness. See the dark as fruitful and nourishing, like a womb. Let this darkness also remind you that all energy has a rhythm of darkness as well as light.

Moving Your Energy with Your Heart

Humans are happiest when they engage from the heart. You know the heart-full experience of holding a precious child, gazing at a loved one, being greeted by a loyal, joyous pet, or embracing the world in meditation.

How much richer your life could be if you learned to expand and extend the list of whom you love! How amazing our world would be if we embraced all living beings, and were embraced by them. As the poet Hafiz wrote, "... Be kind to your sleeping heart. Take it out into the vast fields of Light and let it breathe ..."[8]

Your heart, like all your organs, has an energetic and electromagnetic field. Your radiant heart connects with all of creation. What you store in your heart affects other organs, your cells, your whole body, mind, and spirit. This is why both spiritual teachers and neuroscientists emphasize the importance of forgiveness: by forgiving yourself or another, you are releasing dense, heavy energy that weighs on you, keeps you from feeling connected, and causes ill health. As Brother David Stendl-Rast advised the poet David Whyte, "The prescription for exhaustion is not rest, but whole-heartedness."[9]

Your heart, not your brain, is your primary organ of intelligence. When you expand your heart to connect with everything—qi, the earth, the universe—everything else flows. When you cultivate loving-kindness, Buddhist teacher Pema Chödrön explains,

> ...we train first to be honest, loving, and compassionate toward ourselves. Rather than nurturing self-denigration, we begin to cultivate a clear-seeing kindness. Sometimes we feel good and strong. Sometimes we feel inadequate and weak ... No matter how we feel, we can aspire to be happy. We can learn to act and think in ways that sow seeds of our future well-being, gradually becoming more aware of what causes happiness as well as what causes distress. Without loving-kindness for ourselves, it is difficult, if not impossible, to genuinely feel it for others. [10]

Connecting your heart energy with the heart of the universe is at the center of all heart practices. Américo Yábar expresses it this way,

> In any kind of situation, you have the choice of connecting with the energy that flows in the cosmos. You truly can transform that energy

into love, and bring that love to all of your body. It's very different than "personal power." The important thing is to work with intent and incorporate that cosmic energy transformed in love in order to project that energy to the others. This is the essential principle of the art of magic in the Andes.[11]

HEART COHERENCE

Connect with your heart energy at any time using this practice:

> Shift your attention to your heart. Breathe in and out through your heart. Visualize a person or place you love. Let yourself feel your good feelings as you continue to breathe through your heart.

GRATITUDE

Combine gratitude with breath-and-heart focus to shift your attention:

> Breathe in gratitude through your heart, and breathe out gratitude. Repeat your gratitude breath four times, noticing any changes.

Apply this breath-and-heart focus with any positive emotion, such as:

> Breathe in love, breathe out love.
> Breathe in peace, breathe out peace.
> Breathe in joy, breathe out joy.
> Breathe in harmony, breathe out harmony.

Doing this in a group—at the beginning, the ending, or any time there is group tension—is a wonderful way to shift the energy and reconnect everyone.

ASKING YOUR HEART

Try this when you are faced with a stressful or difficult situation:

> Practice Heart Coherence (above).
> Then ask a question from the heart: "How can I be open-hearted in this situation? Or "What can I do to minimize stress?"
> Listen to the response of your heart. Follow your heart's advice.

TRANSFORMING ENERGY THROUGH YOUR HEART

As with the energetic composting exercises, you are moving energy from one place (inside) to another (outside), and transforming it in this practice:

> Breathe through your heart. Scan your body for any dense or heavy energy.
>
> Imagine rolling the dense energy into a big ball (like a ball of yarn).
>
> Visualize a magic doorway just outside your heart. See the ball of energy moving through the opening, turning to light, and spreading out, lighting the world.

You are becoming more skilled in exchanging energy with the elements, moving energy with your heart, and being in relationship with the living beings around you. You can augment all of these practices with visualization. In the next chapter I invite you to explore visualizing with images, feelings, sensations, and your heart. Playing with holograms of perfection, the qi healing ball, and lines of connection, you will discover wonderful ways to deepen your relationship with earth and cosmos.

CHAPTER 7
CONNECTING
THROUGH VISUALIZATION

To visualize means to see something in your mind's eye, experience it in your body, and sense it in your energy field. Invoking and using hearing, smell, taste, touch, and movement help you create vivid images. Weaving imagination and experience into visualization helps concretize it. Seeing from the heart, as shamans do, helps build connection to what you are visualizing.

Visualizing is a way of training your awareness, concentration, focus, and intent. As you may have noticed, visualizing is an important component of many of the meditations in this book. Once you are able to feel, experience, sense, and see something in your mind's eye and in your heart, you can return to it whenever you like. With practice, it becomes another way to step between the worlds and feed your joy-body.

Visualization is also a tool for allowing unfamiliar perceptions and images into your awareness. For example, the first time you swallow the moon, you might feel you are "making it up." Yet, with practice, the visualization becomes increasingly solid, familiar, and connecting. For many people, unexpected images and sensations—a belly full of starlight, or a felt sense of an animal or otherworldly being next to you—can arise during visualization. All you need to do is accept it and enjoy it. The energy of the unknown is just energy.

In most non-Western cultures, what is being visualized is not a symbol: it is alive, pulsating energy in the larger field, activating the visualizer's felt interconnection with all beings. This is true, for example, of mandalas, Buddhist *thankas*, Shipibo designs on pottery and clothing, Q'ero weavings, Navajo sand paintings, Andean *despachos*, Cro-Magnon cave paintings, and African, Guatemalan, and Balinese dance masks. Like the people in these cultures, you can let your visualizations come alive.

Shifting Your Attention Through Visualization

Visualization is an easy, quick way to shift your attention and help you bring feelings, senses, ideas, and spirit closer together.

When you visualize a clean flowing river, a brilliant galaxy, a snowy mountain peak, or the face of a loved one, you are using your senses, your experience of the person or place, and your heart. The images soothe your brain, relax your body, and create deep connection in the moment.

You can visualize in your car, in the middle of the night, and in the middle of work to remind yourself of what's really important.

Here's an example. Say you are worrying about a friend. You know that worrying does no good, so instead, you purposely imagine that friend surrounded with light—the light of your heart, the light of the divine, the light of the moon, or whatever image comes easily. This shifts your energy from worry to open-heartedness. It sends revitalizing energy to the friend, like a prayer. It creates spacious possibilities for connection to occur. And your intent has a larger impact on the world.

Every time you shift your attention to light or love or beauty, you get better at it. You contribute to the positive-thought index in the world. You feel good and it rubs off on the people around you.

When a baby cries, you naturally move to soothe it, hold it, and connect your two bodies and hearts. Being conscious of how you are soothing yourself as an adult, however, is a challenge. Learning what works to bring you into a more conscious, harmonious state of being is a challenge. Cultural trance is powerful; numbing addictions are rampant. To shift these powerful patterns, you can try one visualization at a time, just as that baby takes one step at a time.

Visualizing Holograms of Possible Perfection

When you visualize, you use imagination, dreaming, and intent to create a mental picture, or hologram. Once created, a hologram can be understood to exist in a parallel reality. Parallel realities are not in competition or conflict with where you are; they simply exist alongside the reality you notice (or think you live in). In every situation, there are choices, and all of them actually play out or manifest in different dimensions.

As you dream, grow, feed, and energize a hologram, your vision affects this "real" world.

"Dreaming" is a tradition that is more than thirty thousand years old. The central belief of the Australian Aborigines is that everything in our world begins in the Dreamtime. Each living thing begins and is incubated in the Dreamtime. After it has become fully developed in the Dreamtime, it then concretizes and becomes a part of our three-dimensional reality. Setting intent is a kind of Dreaming. Alberto Villoldo explains,

> When you access any part of the dream, the great matrix of energy, you can change reality and alter the entire dream ... dreaming the world into being through the very act of witnessing it. Scientists believe that we are only able to do this in the very small, subatomic world. Shamans understand that we also dream the larger world that we experience with our senses. Like the Aborigines, they know that all of creation arises from, and returns to, this dreamtime.[1]

DREAMING A HOLOGRAM OF CLEAN WATER

This mental hologram—visualizing clear, clean, and pure water running everywhere on the earth—is an example of what you can do with visualization. Notice, as you experiment with this practice, how it affects your own consciousness and perception. Be aware, too, that many others around the world are dreaming in this way; your contribution weaves into the larger field of intent for clean, pure water everywhere.

Visualize the groundwater under your feet running clear, clean, and pure. See it filling nearby streams. See the streams running into rivers, also clear, clean, and pure. If you notice debris or toxins in the river, return to your vision of clear, clean, and pure.

Watch the water flow freely. Watch the clear, clean, and pure water spread to nearby lakes, bays, and oceans. See these bodies of water clear, clean, and pure. Keep going: ocean to ocean, continent to continent, until you see all the arteries of the earth's body sparkling clear, clean, and pure.

USING THE QI HEALING BALL

In the ancient Chinese energy practice of *qi gong*, movement and visualization meditations are used to balance and invigorate the body's *qi*—vital, living energy that pervades all forms, both animate and inanimate.

Working with the healing ball is a wonderful practice for learning how to visualize and feel qi, gathering your energy as you do so. Your main focus is to visualize a healing ball and move it through your energetic field and then bring it into your body.[2] As always, you start with intent; as you play with the ball, notice whatever shifts you are experiencing.

Briskly rub your hands together, warming them up for about thirty seconds (this stimulates the meridians). Hold your hands palm to palm, lining up the fingers.

Find the qi ball by pulling your hands away from each other, slowly, until you feel a pushing or a pulling sensation. Trust your senses as your hands find the size of the ball (you will find the size varies day to day, and you can also make it bigger or smaller).

Play with the qi ball by moving your hands closer together and farther apart. Once you get the pushing/pulling sensation going between your hands, you'll get the idea of what the energy field (qi ball) feels like and how to sense it more easily.

Now begin moving the qi ball: to the right and left, above your head and down to your feet, around in circles. Play with it: there's no "right" way to move it. Let the ball be drawn to parts of your body that are sore. Let the ball move in spirals, or in the shape of the infinity symbol, or whatever way it wants to. You are truly engaging your energy with qi energy as you do this.

After a while—when it feels right—bring the ball into your body, holding the outer edge of the qi ball against your skin with your hands. Continue to move the ball inside you, bringing it to your internal organs, a sore shoulder, a bad knee. Play with it, noticing what happens.

When you feel complete, gather your energy by raising your hands over your head and bringing them down to your belly. Hold them here and then put your right hand on your heart, aligning belly and heart energy. Next raise your right hand to your third eye, aligning heart and third eye energy. Bend and place your hands on the ground, releasing any excess energy to the earth.

Playing with and moving the qi ball for five minutes a day helps you gather, move, and smooth energy in both the physical and etheric planes. Connecting with qi automatically does the energetic work of filling and connecting. It also stretches your limbs in every direction without your having to think "exercise."

VISUALIZING LINES OF CONNECTION

Coloring books for young children used to have images made of dots. The child's task was to "connect the dots" by drawing lines between them, so the whole picture could emerge. Sometimes the dots were numbered to reinforce counting and orderly behavior; sometimes they were just dots on the page.

Developing conscious, intentional, loving connection with what-ever is in our environment is an energetic version of connecting the dots. It builds "mental muscle memory," writes David Spangler.[3] By connecting ourselves regularly to the living energy around us, and feeding the joy-body, we train ourselves to assume connection. In connection, we feel less alone, more supported, and more alive as a part of the whole.

Doing this kind of visualization regularly means that, in times of stress or pain, we can switch gears: renewing connection, and not abandoning ourselves or another to hopelessness and fear.

CONNECTING THE DOTS:
TAKING A MOMENT OF LOVE

"People talk about taking a 'moment of silence.' I think of this practice as taking a moment of Love," says Spangler.[4] I have modified his description of this simple visualization so you can explore it for yourself:

Begin by seeing a line of love and appreciation between yourself and an object. Appreciate this object for what it is. No matter what other feelings are present, simply allow the connection of love and appreciation between the two of you.

Broaden your focus. Allow your sense of loving connection and appreciation to expand, embracing other objects around you and the room itself.

Notice that the lines of connection, love, and appreciation between you and the objects become lines of connection between the objects themselves. Make this explicit.

Ask that as your love expands out into the room and beyond, everything it touches discovers its connection with everything else. Let the love connect the dots.

Notice the sense of wholeness that emerges in the room. It becomes more that a room full of objects of varying sizes, shapes, materials, and uses. It becomes an energetic "ecosystem" in its own right.

USING VISUALIZATION TO DEEPEN
YOUR CONNECTION WITH AN ELEMENT

Over the years as I have worked with the practices in this book, I have been amazed by the deepening that visualization provides. I've explored and played with what would happen as I added images to my repertoire. The fire meditation visualization that follows is an example of how you can feed your experience of living in the heart of the universe.

Open your heart to the sun. Breathe out your heavy energy, gifting it to the sun. Visualize and breathe the fire, the heat, and the transformative power of the sun into your heart, filling yourself. Repeat.

Continue to breathe out your heavy energy, gifting it now to the spiritual sun behind the sun.[5] Visualize and breathe the potential of the sun behind the sun into your heart, filling yourself. Repeat.

Continue to breathe out your heavy energy, gifting it now to a specific star (I use Sirius because I have a relationship with it). Visualize and breathe the radiance and power of the star into your heart, filling yourself. Repeat.

Continue to breathe out your heavy energy, gifting it now to a galaxy (I use Andromeda). Visualize and breathe the massive energy of the galaxy into your heart, filling yourself. Repeat.

Continue to breathe out your heavy energy, gifting it now to the center of the universe. Visualize and breathe the universe's potential for creation and destruction into your heart, filling yourself. Repeat.

As you can see, visualization offers limitless expansion of the ways you can connect with earth and cosmos.

VISUALIZING CONNECTION: THE BUSHMAN WAY

A very few Bushman people in Southern Africa still live as hunter-gatherers in an extremely demanding desert environment.[6]

The beautiful Naro San Bushman way of teaching "directional bonding" to their children is a model that expands on Connecting the Dots: Taking a Moment of Love. As tracker Jon Young describes the practice, when the very youngest children begin to notice a bird, they are taught to create a *thread* of connection to it—observing its habits, learning its name and sounds. As they age, accompanying adults in gathering and hunting, they learn more: the specific sounds of mating and danger, the location of nests and food sources, and habits of living. This awareness helps the child create a *string* of connection to the bird. As the child matures, she creates a *cord*, and later a *rope* to the bird, knowing everything about its behavior, and being in relationship with it as part of the living energy that surrounds the tribal grouping. Such directional bonding grows naturally with all beings the Bushmen share their environment with—trees, rivers, animals, plants, clouds, insects, soil, seasons.[7] They live, as Thich Nhat Hanh and Joanna Macy speak of it, in a state of "interbeing."

Directional bonding is one way of describing what all our indigenous ancestors did: observe, connect, merge, and live as equal, reciprocal beings in the whole environment. North American Plains people speak of "all our relations" to characterize this way of living.

We know from DNA sequencing that we are all, in fact, relatives. All humans are genetically descended from the Bushmen people and thirteen other "ancestral population clusters" in Africa.

This suggests that we have similar capabilities "in our bones," that we can breathe through our ancestors, opening space and time, to remember how to live in reciprocal connection, perception, and awareness despite centuries of disconnect. We can enlarge our vision, and plant that vision in our own soil, our own bioregion. We can vision and make new stories of community and directional bonding.

Visualizing augments your ability to engage somatically with living energy and develop your felt sense of interbeing. In the next chapter, I invite you to incorporate and build on your relationship with places you love on the earth, integrating visualization into the central "Meditation with the Earth and the Cosmos" (page 113).

Chapter 8
Meditating with
the Earth and the Cosmos

When you *assume* you are connected—with a person, group, local creek, sacred place, animal, or the earth—your perception changes. When you build on your connections, your perception deepens.

Each time you connect with a place—whether physically or in dream, shamanic journey, or meditation—your relationship expands.[1] Resonance with other dreamers from other times feeds your sense of wholeness and your connection with the unseen.

By repeatedly visualizing a field of awareness between yourself, the earth, and the cosmos; with your local mountains, rivers, bays, and watershed; with places of power—mountains, standing stones, the still-revered spiritual places of the Old Ones; and beyond to the cosmos, you can experience yourself as both an integral and tiny part of a very large universe. The practice of connecting, receiving, expanding, breathing, and merging with the energies of a place is a way for you to return awareness and consciousness to yourself-as-part-of-the-whole.

Indigenous people feed their energetic connections to place with offerings, ceremony, altars, meditation, and pilgrimage. It is natural to maintain relationship with the land that sustains you in every way.

It is not hard for us to take up these practices again, in small and large ways. Doing this changes us. Finding our own personal resonance with places that are sacred to us, whether backyard tree or ancient monument, helps us heal our own hearts and find our place within the heart of the cosmos.

Developing Connective Filaments with Places You Love

Meditation with the Earth and the Cosmos offers you a way to connect regularly and deeply with places you love: the creek you played in as a child, the mountain you climbed, the ancient sacred places you have visited.

Practicing this meditation helps you develop your perception, bringing you into alignment, reciprocity, resonance, and receptivity. It helps you strengthen the multidirectional energetic filaments between yourself and place. It also roots you between the earth and the cosmos, like the Tree of Life that appears in cultures around the world.

This meditation is a key practice for shifting your vibration and anchoring yourself in the times to come. As you align yourself with the energies of heaven and earth, your cells become vehicles in the larger patterns of cosmic balance and resonance. The meditation will help you meet the changes in the world with power, fluidity, and balance.

With consistent practice, you will feel the energies physically, and you will notice that they are in fact always flowing through your body, always available for connection and healing. Because the stars and supernovas are composed of the same elements as your body and our planet, you have a natural resonance with both earth and cosmos. The fountain of energy that moves between them is inexhaustible, so you can always connect with it and draw upon it.

Moreover, you mirror the actual filaments in the universe with this meditation: the "cosmic web," formed of sheets and filaments of dark matter, is a "web-like pattern that pervades and gives structure to the universe."[2]

The meditation is broken into parts so you can learn the simple pattern of heart alignment first. When you are ready, you can expand the pattern to connect with places you love, have visited, and want a relationship with.

MEDITATION WITH THE EARTH AND THE COSMOS: HEART ALIGNMENT

To begin, sit or lie quietly with your eyes closed. Take long, slow breaths, making inhalation and exhalation equal, slowing down until you feel each part of each breath. Slowing your breathing helps you focus your attention. Become aware of the energy entering your crown, passing through your body, and going down out of the base of your spine into the earth. This energy is moving through you all the time, and it is wonderfully connecting to notice it. When you are breathing deeply and calmly, repeat each part of the following three-part sequence at least four times:

#1 Celestial

As you inhale, bring celestial energies—stars, planets, galaxies, universes—down through your crown chakra to your heart. Mix your heart energy with the celestial energies and, as you exhale, send all into the earth through your root chakra or your feet. Do this four times.

#2 Terrestrial

As you inhale, bring terrestrial energies up from the earth through your root chakra or feet to your heart. Mix your heart energy with the terrestrial energies and, as you exhale, send all out through your crown chakra into the cosmos. Do this four times.

You become a conduit for the energies to flow as you build this pillar between earth and cosmos.

#3 Integrating Self, Earth, and Cosmos

As you inhale, bring both celestial and terrestrial energies into your heart.

As you exhale, mix your heart energy with the terrestrial and celestial energies, and send all the energies out from your heart in every direction: to your cells, your bones and blood, your luminous energy field, and beyond, in constantly expanding three-dimensional spheres. Do this four times.

Notice how much you feel like a tree, with your roots in the ground and your branches in the sky.

MEDITATION WITH THE EARTH AND THE COSMOS: EXPANDING YOUR CONNECTIONS

Once you are comfortable creating the heart alignment (earth to heart to cosmos), you can further explore your connections with places that are sacred to you. Try extending your filaments into your home, your land, your sacred mountains, rivers and lakes, your bioregion, and other places you love around the earth. Visualize the details of places where you have walked, made offerings, camped, or played. Feel them in your heart. Practice *sending and receiving* these energies in and through your body.

Feed the webs of connection—ley lines, earth chords, *ceke* lines, earth and star grids—by visualizing energetic filaments running *from* your earth-cosmos-connected heart *to and from* the place you are visualizing, and from each place to the next, creating strong energetic and visual connections.[3] In the process you will be helping to reweave and repair the earth grids and webs of life. You will strengthen your own connections within the web.

For example, eight mountains around the San Francisco Bay Area where I live were sacred to indigenous people; they are also sacred to many of us in the present. Ceremony, pilgrimage, and offerings fill these mountains still. Meditation with the Earth and the Cosmos provides a way for us to stay in heart contact with the mountains even when we cannot be physically on them. By integrating our physical experiences, recollections of ceremony, and perceptions of place into our visualizations, we keep the energy and sacredness of the mountains alive in our hearts and our spiritual practices.

#1 Expanding to a Place You Love

Continue to inhale celestial and terrestrial energies into your heart.

As you exhale, send a thread of these energies out from your heart to a place you love. Draw the energy of that place back into your heart. Repeat, until you feel a strong filament of connection between you and your place.

Repeat this with as many places as you want, drawing your web of connections into your heart and out again.

For example, one of the places I connect with daily is Mt. Tamalpais, north of San Francisco. Each time I send my heart filament to the mountain, I visualize a different aspect of it: the peak, where I have made many *despacho* offerings; the huge hilltop serpentine mass looking out on the Pacific Ocean, San Francisco Bay, and Mt. Diablo to the east; the creek trail that winds down the whole mountain to the sea; the base of the mountain where it touches the ocean; and the west-facing trail that winds through sunlight and shadow, streambeds and dry hills. These places where my feet have touched the mountain hold energy, memory, and experience, all of which are woven into the images and my connection.

#2 Weaving a Web of Connection

Choose three or four more places to connect with.

Repeat the pattern for each place you are connecting with: inhale celestial and terrestrial energies into your heart, send them from your heart to the next place, and draw the energy of that place back into your heart.

Visualize as much as you can of the place—where you have hiked, how it looks from a distance, the day you found a special wildflower, the day a storm caught you—and see the filament of connection moving back and forth from your heart to each place.

As you expand your web of connections, feel the whole of them in your heart and all your cells. Rest in this awareness.

#3 Creating a Field of Consciousness

Repeat the meditation daily, connecting with the same sacred places each day. Maintaining connection with places sacred to you is a powerful way to build relationship and establish a field of consciousness, a field of awareness.

As you visualize each place, learn its energies. Let yourself experience those energies somatically and spiritually. Learn what the place is teaching you. Listen to the messages. Empower yourself with them.

For example, the energy of a mountain may teach you to be "solid and present," call you to do ceremony there, or show you how you are "connected to the bones of all the other mountains." You might use the energy of one lake to release what does not serve you, and another to "dive into your own light." An ancient sacred boulder might teach you to explore the past with the Old Ones, or to experience the void. These relationships are a mystery; what we are led to in relationship with each place is particular to us, and to our paths in the world.

Just as Aboriginal songs recreate the land, Meditation with the Earth and the Cosmos helps us create a field of consciousness through our intent, resonance, and connection.[4]

Extending Your Practice: Personal and Global Healing

The Meditation with the Earth and the Cosmos is a vehicle for calming the mind, body, and nervous system. It is a powerful energy-shifting practice.

Doing short repetitions of the meditation during the day helps you shift your focus from the mundane to the sacred. Doing it in the middle of the night when you cannot sleep is a way to calm, center, and reconnect yourself with what matters. Doing it daily helps you weave the physical and the energetic, the mundane and the sacred. It may give you a sense of dissolving, or mixing with everything. It will certainly give you a deeper connection with all that is.

Over the years I have asked my student apprentices how they use the meditation. Moria says,

> *I use Meditation with the Earth and the Cosmos to change my head, to interrupt a heavy mental state and ground, center, and return to my heart and my connections with the greater Web. It feels very nourishing to me, and to the land.*
>
> *Recently, I've also used it as part of healing work, drawing the energies both through myself and through the subject, letting those energies of stars and earth rebuild and repair where they may. So for me in those two examples, it's really about the Web, and the connection of all that is, branches to roots.*

Performing this meditation at sacred sites opens doorways to deep knowledge.

Doing this meditation outdoors, connected to the earth, helps you learn to feel and embody the various energy fields of the earth.

Doing the meditation daily gives you a way to make a prayer for the earth. In turn, those places you love will give back to you in reciprocity: the mountain may support you on your long hike. The river may appear to you in a stressful situation, reminding you of fluidity. The sacred stone may guide you. The star beings may come down to you and influence your work, as they did with the Old Ones and do now with ordinary people.[5] Another apprentice, Carol, tells me,

> *Meditation with the Earth and the Cosmos expands my awareness into formless forms. Sometimes it is quite visual, showing me places, or Spirit Beings I had not yet met. At other times, it gives more of a feeling-sense experience, taking me to meet and merge with others (Trees, Mountains, Unseen Beings, and so on) for developing and extending relationships with them.*

Over time and with practice, the meditation changes your vibrational energy and cellular structure, enabling you to meet these times with reconfigured and fluid energy, and to be an anchor for others who are less connected. It helps you create a feeling of sanctuary, timeless and holy. Linea, another apprentice, says,

> *The meditation helps me feel my deep connection to this planet, the strength I get from the earth, and the spaciousness of the Universe as the true Source of my Being. It has helped me flow through some very difficult situations without being overwhelmed by them, and with the capacity to bring peace and joy through myself and to others.*

WEAVING FILAMENTS OF HEALING

The principle of building energetic connection with place can be applied to areas of natural and human disaster. Grounding and focusing yourself first, you can visualize energetic filaments running from your earth-cosmos-connected heart to a person, group, or place that needs healing, just as people still do in the Peruvian Andes.

Because we are all interconnected, we all experience what happens around the earth. As Thich Nhat Hanh said after the Indian Ocean tsunami in 2004, "... suffering is a collective matter. What happens in one part of the body happens to the whole. We have all died ..."

Doing the meditation helps you move out of "small self" or ego as you experience your interconnectedness with all life, and move from the personal to the communal. The more you practice it, the more you strengthen your ability to focus your intent on embodying, loving, and caring for the whole of creation.

Claudia, an apprentice from many years ago, explains,

Meditation with the Earth and the Cosmos is a way to help me ground in my body, move out of my head, and be in my heart. It is a vehicle to connect with energies outside the constrictions of time and space, and ultimately helps me feel part of all that is. It moves me from small-mind thinking to a much greater perspective, relieving stress and anxiety based on the illusion of separation. I have passed this practice on to many of my clients over the years who suffer from anxiety. With regular practice, it can shift my whole day; my energy field feels brighter, expanded, and in alignment.

Adding my own heart consciousness to the mix of earth and celestial energies reminds me that we are in a reciprocal relationship with all living beings.

It reminds me to breathe, feel my feet on mother earth, and know I am connected to the vastness of the entire universe.

Masaru Emoto echoes these possibilities for healing in writing about his research with water crystals:

... I have proven that people's pure energy of consciousness can change the water in areas that people have prayed for, regardless of the distance ... the most effective prayer is the feeling of Love and Thanks.[6]

How a Relationship Builds: Apu Ausangate

For those who grow up on the land, relationship is embedded: in language, story, daily practice, cosmology, and spiritual and cultural assumptions. For the rest of us, such ineffable relationships grow over time with intent, resonance, reciprocity, receptivity, and practice.

Often what becomes important is revealed slowly in seemingly random but synchronous events. Our task is to pay attention, listen for messages both mundane and sacred, and make the connections.

I trace my relationship with the sacred Andean mountain Ausangate to a series of experiences that developed over a ten-year period. The mountain loomed large in my imagination: it is central to the Q'eros with whom I was experiencing living energy and learning ceremony. On my second trip to the Andes, I was gifted with a small peaked stone; the giver said "Ausangate" to me. The stone looked like the mountain, came from the mountain, and began my physical connection with it. On the same trip, while I was waffling about buying another "ordinary" (for daily use) handwoven alpaca poncho from my Q'ero friend Fernando, he said, "Buy it and you will return to visit Ausangate!" Despite being unable to imagine doing that with a young child at home, I bought the poncho.

Next, a friend made me an essence (a vibrational remedy) of the Ausangate stone. I often put a drop of the essence on my crown chakra. The mountain began appearing in my shamanic journeys; I traveled there in nonordinary reality to explore and learn. I added Ausangate to my daily Meditation with the Earth and the Cosmos.

After about eight years, I began to dream of visiting Ausangate in person. I searched for guided trips, found one, and signed up. After a week in Cusco, during which many in the group got sick, we began our journey into the mountains. By the time we arrived at our starting point, I had bacterial bronchitis and was too weak to walk to our 17,500-foot destination. Our guide, Jose Luis Herrera, procured a beautiful black *Paso* (Peruvian horse) for me to ride. I was grateful, and it was strange: for someone who always has her feet on the ground, I was suddenly traveling above ground, head in the clouds, unrooted.

At base camp, I collapsed and slept as soon as the tents were up. That became my pattern: join the group for side trips to lagoons and sacred waterways, then sleep fourteen hours each day. Normally I would have been running around, exploring the mountain, finding stones, seeing everything I could, but I was too sick.

When I returned home, it came to me: I had drawn in the energy of the mountain, through my body and bones, as I slept those fourteen hours on the earth each day. I didn't have a lot of visions or adventures, but I *felt* the energy of the mountain. Now, when I connect with Ausangate in my Meditation with the Earth and the Cosmos, my body resonates with the mountain's solidity, power, and presence. I become the mountain. The mountain becomes me.

Now that you know how to use meditation and visualization to connect yourself in dialogue with anywhere you love, any place you see as sacred, the next chapter will bring you back to your immediate surroundings. I invite you to step back from mountains and into the forest, learning to develop reciprocal relationships with the trees, plants, and creatures that surround your everyday world.

Chapter 9
Deepening Your Energetic Connections with Your Surroundings

You live in a matrix of living, vibrating energy. Engaging and connecting with this matrix, with the living energy of all things, is a deeply rewarding and mystical journey.

As your experience of energetic connectedness grows, your heart fills. Your engagement with all of the living beings and energy fields that surround you expands naturally. You are less prone to being sidetracked by density, whether inside or outside you. You are more fluid and better able to recover from illness, despair, and immobility. Your sense of separation diminishes as your engagement with human, natural, and elemental forces grows. You are better able to focus on being present with what is, and to envision the world you want to live in—"the more beautiful world our hearts know is possible," as Charles Eisenstein so eloquently put it.[1]

When you experience your energy connected with all living beings, it is as if your heart has no boundaries. In this field of consciousness, light and energy flow in all directions; you receive as well as give, basking in your luminous becoming. You discover, as so many ancient spiritual traditions have done, that in resonance there is no other. You experience union.

The Effects
of Opening and Expanding

When you have established an energetic, heartfelt connection with nature—whether with mountain, bobcat, lake, or a tree planted along a city sidewalk—repeating your practice takes you directly to the energy of the connection. The practice can be meditation or movement, visualization or song—it does not matter. Energy builds and spirals: practice leads to connection; connection leads to stronger practice; stronger practice leads to deeper connection. This connection shows you that you are not alone. It helps you step out of your small self and into an expanded sense of relationship in the world. It helps you live in your joy-body.

Your energy practice can give you, as my student Samantha expresses it,

> ... *courage to walk in new ways in old places, and courage to find and be in new places that are waiting to be explored. My connection to source, the ancestors, and our mother the earth has deepened.*

Developing
Reciprocal Relationships

Developing a relationship with any other living being is similar to creating a friendship. You engage and explore. You spend time together. You talk. You give gifts. You negotiate. You ask questions. You ask for help, or give it. You appreciate each other.

Children do this naturally, with trees, rocks, animals, and other "imaginary friends," if they are given any chance to be outside. Some adults manage to remember the power of these relationships, and keep them up. At the same time, jobs, families, and life demands intervene. Those around you may be oblivious to, befuddled by, or hostile to your desire to be outside and connected, so you lose heart. Cultural belief in hierarchy, separateness, and abstract concepts leads you to doubt that you can have real relationships with nonhuman living beings.

Yet by exploring your actual *sensory, experiential,* and *imaginal* perceptions, you can develop and deepen such relationships. You are not thinking up interpretations with your ordinary mind; you're allowing yourself to *be* and *listen deeply* in order to *perceive* and *experience*. When you consider that only 7 percent of human communication is verbal, it becomes easier to imagine coming into congruence with other living beings.

The Japanese practice of Forest Therapy *(shinrin-yoku)*—feeling the wind and sunshine on your skin, listening to insects and birds, touching stones, bark, and leaves, always with gratitude—exemplifies such calming, reciprocal relationships.[2]

As Norwegian Morten Wolf Storeide, founder of the World Drum Project tells us,

We do not have to learn the language of Mother Earth. We are all born with it, we all carry it and we all know it, we only have to remember it. Then we can listen and then we can respect what we all are a part of.[3]

Making Friends with a Tree: Deep Listening

If you grew up around trees, your body remembers the ones you climbed or read under, swung from, or used for imaginary games. It is not hard: to make relationships with a tree you are drawn to, you only have to drop your adult self-consciousness and judgment. That might mean leaning up against an ancient oak during a hike, or lying along the low branch of one. It might mean circling the biggest tree in your neighborhood, drawing your fingertips across its bark daily to say hello. Or it might mean painting a picture of the tree, bringing it offerings, singing to it, or becoming its caretaker.

Deep listening is a way of being fully present with what is happening in the moment without trying to control it or judge it. You let go of your inner clamoring and your usual assumptions. You listen actively, with respect, openness, and spaciousness, to hear precisely what is being said. Deep listening is an ongoing practice of suspending self-oriented, reactive thinking and opening your awareness to the unknown, unexpected, and mysterious.

The process of deep listening to a tree begins with your sensory, physical engagement with the tree itself. Slowly, as you become familiar and make friends, you notice more: the birds and other creatures that move through the tree; how wind and sun interact with it; patterns of light and shadow; how the tree interacts with other trees nearby. Then you make perceptual shifts, open your cells, and experience the energy field that surrounds you and the tree, the tree and its neighbors, the ecosystem it is a part of. As you notice these energies and interactions, your relationship comes alive.

The physical plays into metaphysical: it is easier to journey to the magical realms a tree inhabits when you have a relationship in the sensory world. All the childhood stories you read where a hole in a tree was the opening used to enter magical other worlds are based on this. This method—visionary perception, seeing from the heart, and exploring what is not visible to the eyes (shamanism)—is at least fifty thousand years old.

Your process of making friends with a tree (and any other living being) grows with interaction, relationship, ceremony, and longevity. Your intent to have a relationship, and to honor your tree, feeds the whole.[4]

As I was writing this book, I asked Mother Oak, a 350-year-old Coast Live Oak behind my former house, to explain perception to me. This is part of what she replied:

Your perception began with your making a physical relationship with me. You visited me. You circled me, touching my bark. You used my bark for your clay projects. You brought others to me, all of you rattling, encircling, making a connection with me. You made ceremony with me, gave me offerings, and brought others to give offerings to me.

Each time you came our relationship deepened. Each time you engaged your perception expanded: you began to feel my connection through the roots with other trees. You began to notice my connection through branches with the other trees, with the plants in the field, with the

*ecosystem around us. Your perception grew with our relationship and
our reciprocal conversation.*

THICH NHAT HANH: SMILING WITH TREES

Buddhist monk, poet, and peace activist Thich Nhat Hanh, exiled from
his homeland of Vietnam in 1973, describes dreaming the same dream
for a year: seeing a beautiful hill he recalled from his native land and
being prevented by obstacles from climbing it. When he visited a new
place and was homesick, he writes,

> *I knew I could go outside, in the backyard or to a park, and find a
> place to practice breathing and smiling under the trees... I know that
> in our previous lives we were trees, and even in this life we continue
> to be trees. Without trees, we cannot have people, therefore trees and
> people inter-are. We are trees, and air, bushes, and clouds. If trees
> cannot survive, humankind is not going to survive either..."[5]*

Thich Nhat Hanh goes on to describe a doctor in New York City
who gives the same prescription to many patients, telling them "You
are sick because you are cut off from Mother Nature." This is the prescription, which you also can use:

> *Each morning, take a bus and go to the tree in the center of the city
> and practice tree-hugging. You hug the tree and you breathe in saying,
> "I am with my mother," and you breathe out saying, "I am happy." And
> you look at the tree so green, and smell the bark of the tree so fragrant.[6]*

TREE METAPHOR, MYTH, AND ENTRAINMENT

You can draw on your relationships with actual trees as you learn to
be like them in the midst of this changing world. You can see your
roots spreading, connecting with other roots, drawing nutrients from
the soil. You can pull those nutrients up through your body (trunk)
and out your crown (branches), reaching toward your potential. You
can draw in light and energy from the stars and galaxies, just as trees

do. You can mimic trees' continual movement of energy, nurturing yourself from the ground you inhabit and breathing in the fresh air (oxygen) that trees offer you.

You can also draw on the mythic, cross-cultural images of the world tree to remind yourself of your alignment with heaven and earth, and of your interconnected and symbiotic relationships. The world tree offers you a way to embrace the whole.

Some years ago soundscape recorder Bernie Krause performed a wonderful experiment that offers insight into how other living beings respond to humans.[7] In the experiment, long-time meditators sat with their backs to trees and entered a meditative state. Using highly sensitive recording devices, Krause measured the rhythms of both human breath and tree sap rising and falling. Each tree slowed the flow of its sap to match the breathing pattern of its meditator. The trees *consciously entrained* with the humans.

Touching or hugging trees affects your biological and vibrational health.[8] You can teach yourself to entrain with a tree by letting your breath, your consciousness, and your awareness match the tree's awareness, and by listening to tree's music, story, advice, and requests.

Rejuvenating Yourself in an Urban Environment

When it comes to doing transformative practices, my clients often tell me, "I don't have time." I understand this well: as a working single mom raising my daughter, I was lucky to find an hour a week to myself. Yet even in that context I found ways to be outside, connect with nature, and rejuvenate myself at work. This section is devoted to readers who are busy with jobs, families, and life—and especially you urban dwellers.

The tools you have been learning—breathing, visualizing, noticing, and building your connections through meditation—can be applied to urban creatures, plants in your office, weeds in an empty lot, and the single tree shading your outside eating area at work. If deepening your connections is important to you, you can find ways no matter where you are.

Bring Nature into Your Environment

When you want to shift your awareness and focus away from the mundane concerns of life, bringing rocks, plants, crystals, or any symbol of nature into your home, workplace, or pocket can help you shift your attention.

When I had to visit a difficult relative, I learned to carry a small, smooth rose quartz crystal in my pocket, fingering it so I could remember there was a world beyond. When my mother was in a residential care facility and extremely anxious, I used an old oak outside her window to calm myself down so I could be patient with her. When I lived in snow country, I kept houseplants so I could observe living things even in winter.

These practices may seem super obvious, yet it is surprising how many of us forget, or become habituated to rather barren environments. Even just having plants in a workplace increases productivity by 15 percent! Think of how your life could improve if you nurtured your own office plant and learned to listen to it!

USING A STONE TO RECONNECT

Find a stone you like during a walk on the beach, or while on vacation. Study its surroundings as you put it in your pocket, memorizing its home ecosystem and natural environment.

When you return home, keep the stone on your desk. Let the stone be a connector to your memories of the place. Use the stone to step outside of where you are (an office, an apartment) and into that other world. As you do this, your fluidity will improve, and you will learn to step between the two worlds. Using the lines of connection between you and the stone's home place will shift your perception.

Like visualizing the face of a loved one, visualizing a specific part of the natural world helps you shift into heart fullness and your joy-body. Even when you cannot physically connect, you can use your memories to nourish yourself.

FIND RESPITE FROM THE OFFICE

My first full-time job was in a huge government office building in Washington, DC. These were pre-cubicle days, so I actually shared an office that had a door. But I was used to being outside, and I felt suffocated in that office. I learned to bring my lunch so I could take time to walk in the nearby parks.

Later, I was working in a suburban law office when I discovered that about five blocks away was an old dirt road leading to a creek. I could scramble down that road, and sitting beside the water I discovered polliwogs and blue herons, crawdads (a sign of healthy water), and old trees. Spending my lunch hour next to that creek gave me back my sanity.

The same thing happened when I went to work in Silicon Valley. Unhappy breathing stale air and being surrounded by type-A personalities, I found another nearby creek I visited at least once a week. One day a deer walked by. Another day I saw a kingfisher, a beautiful, elusive fishing bird who darts up and down waterways. I watched watersliders and minnows, letting the stress slide away as I shifted my focus, my breath, and my whole being in the presence of these alive, wild creatures. You can do the same.

FINDING YOUR SPECIAL PLACE

Find a park, a creek, or a semi-wild place near your office. Visit on your lunch hour. Explore until you find a tree where you can rest your back, or an interesting hideaway. Let yourself come into stillness, simply observing whatever surrounds you. Let your ears fill with the sounds that surround you, and let your skin feel the breeze. Even if you are sitting next to some scruffy plants, let yourself notice the interactions taking place: bees and bugs, ants and beetles, small chirping birds, whatever comes into the plant. Let yourself enter the world that surrounds you.

The more you focus outside of yourself, the more your worries will drop away and you will experience yourself as part of the larger world. Then, once you have become familiar with your special place, you can bring it to mind wherever you are—just as I can vividly recall the kingfisher from thirty-five years ago.

STUDYING WEEDS

"The moment one gives close attention to anything, even a blade of grass, it becomes a mysterious, awesome, indescribably magnificent world in itself," said Henry Miller.[9]

I was once at a silent meditation retreat where we were instructed not to hike, do yoga, or engage in any active pursuits. The purpose of this was to help us stay aware and within ourselves, avoiding sensory distraction. At meals outside, I sat on the same piece of ground next to some common weeds every day. Tasting and chewing my food without talking was a good practice of awareness, and in the silence those weeds drew my attention. They taught me a wonderful lesson: I did not need to rush around hiking every surrounding trail and exploring the terrain. Instead, zoning into those weeds became fascinating. The way they smelled, swayed in the breeze, and shifted appearance in different light became my entire world. My awareness of what was possible in stillness expanded. Try this:

> Find a patch of weeds outside your house or office. Visit them daily, and make friends. Sit beside them and say hello. Observe the bugs climbing on them and the soil they grow in. Notice how this changes your awareness.

TAKE A MINI-VACATION FROM ELECTRONICS

Some people travel to get themselves out of their ruts, their habitual ways of being. Others take a "spa day" or hike ten miles.

Another, less expensive way to take a break from whatever path you are on is to take a mini-vacation from all your electronic devices. As part of a wired society, this might be a challenge for you; and you will discover amazing results: clarity about how you distract yourself, insights into alternative ways of being, and calmness as you replace a frenetic activity with slower ones. This mini-vacation is an opportunity to practice all you have been learning about releasing heaviness and filling with lighter, different energy.

TAKING A MINI-VACATION FROM ELECTRONICS

Try this for one whole day, or even three days:

> Put your mobile devices—cell, computer, tablet, anything else you rely on constantly—away. Let your mind rest in breath and your body in movement: take a slow, conscious walk, breathing in fresh air, releasing tension. Practice releasing and filling with all the elements. Any time your mind panics and tells you to check your mobile, breathe out that heavy notion and breathe in some lighter energy. Continue using releasing-and-filling practices all day, observing how they help you shift your attention and calm your body/mind.

Drawing on your immediate surroundings to deepen your energetic connections gives you yet another way to develop reciprocal relationships. In the next chapter, I invite you to expand your practices with sound, vibration, silence, meditation, and movement.

CHAPTER 10
OPENING YOUR HEART WITH SOUND, MEDITATION, AND SILENCE

You live in a universe of harmonic vibration. Each living being vibrates to precise frequencies and uses sound to communicate. As Bernie Krause explains,

> *Every living organism—from the tiniest to the largest—and every site on earth has its own acoustic signature ... What reaches out to us from the wild is a deeply profound connection—a constantly evolving multidimensional weave of sonic fabric.*[1]

Everything—a human body, a landscape, the Earth herself—has a healthy, resonant frequency. Every human (not just babies!) also has a unique, individual tone that you can identify across the room or in a crowd. Masaru Emoto's photographs of water crystals changing shape—in response to sound and written words—give visible form to what all living beings experience.[2]

The words, vibrations, and sounds you emit affect your body, the fields around you, and the world. With conscious choice, you can use the vibrations of sound, breath, and silence to release the heavy, bring in the light, expand your connection, and shift the energy you emanate. This can make a huge difference in your health and in the happiness of those around you.

Sound and Vibration

Vibration comes from sound as well as other forms of energy, such as movement and light: think of the vibration of hummingbird wings, the vibration of thunder, rain, and earthquake, the vibration of your cranial-sacral fluid. Every vibration resonates in your physical and energy body, in the air, and in material things in ever-widening circles like a tossed stone's ripples in water.

The resonant (and dissonant) effects of sound and vibration are familiar to you. Think about how your body responds to birdsong and cricket chirping; to radio talk shows; to an explosion; to Beethoven, Indian raga, didgeridoo, or Wagner; to constant urban background noise; to a beloved's voice. A song can lift your spirit or bring tears to your eyes. A chant can open your heart, give you courage, or draw you into relaxation. Your heart's intent, heard through the vibrations of your voice, has far more impact on the listener than your words. Harsh words (and the energy behind them) can cause heaviness in individuals, families, and nations.

Many cultures draw on their vast bodies of wisdom about the vibrational qualities of everything—plants, stones, stories, elements, foods, sound, and light—and how those qualities affect organs, systems, emotions, energy, and spiritual states of mind. Curanderismo, Ayurveda, homeopathic, and plant and herbal medicine all draw on such vibrational wisdom. For example, the vibrations associated with foods in the Ayurvedic tradition are known to affect both the physical and spiritual body.

In Sanskrit, one of the earliest Asian languages and an ancestor of Indo-European tongues, every sound was understood to send a particular energy into the universe. Sounds, words, and chants were used with precision and intent to create and affect energetic states, and to interact with the whole harmonic creation. Quechua, Hindu, and Buddhist devotional chanting are similar.

In the overtone chanting of the Mongolian steppes and the *Kai* throat singing of the Siberian Altai, vibration is used as a vehicle for coming into resonance and connecting and communicating with physical and spiritual landscapes.[3] In Mayan languages in Central America, the vibrational beauty of the words people use is central to maintaining the fabric of community and the daily work of weaving the world together. The rhythm and melodic contour of Aboriginal songlines describe the nature of the land over which the song passes; walking on the songline and observing the land are the same as listening to the song.

GEOMETRIC AND VIBRATIONAL PATTERNS OF ENERGY: THE SHIPIBO

Shipibo practice models the possibilities of vibrational awareness. On the Upper Amazon, the Shipibo people use a complex weaving of vibration and design, the acoustic and the visual, to create harmony in the physical world and engage in dialogue with the spirit world. Howard G. Charing's story gives a sense of how this works:

> *The Shipibo can listen to a song or chant by looking at the [pottery and cloth] designs, and inversely paint a pattern by listening to a song or music.*

> *As an astonishing demonstration of this I witnessed two Shipiba paint a large ceremonial ceramic pot known as a Mahuete. The pot was nearly five feet high and had a diameter of about three feet. Each of the Shipiba couldn't see what the other was painting, yet both were whistling the same song, and when they had finished, both sides of the complex geometric pattern were identical and matched each side perfectly.[4]*

The ethnologist Angelika Gebhart-Sayer calls this "visual music." The patterns express oneness, harmony, and a union or fusion of perceived opposites (complementarity) extending beyond the borders of the pottery or cloth and permeating the entire world.

Charing goes on to say that

> *In the deep ayahuasca trance, the [sacred plant] reveals to the shaman the luminous geometric patterns of energy. These filaments drift*

towards the mouth of the shaman where it metamorphoses into a chant or icaro. The icaro is a conduit for the patterns of creation which permeate the body of the shaman's patient bringing harmony ... Speaking personally ... this is a feeling that every cell in my body is floating and embraced in a nurturing all-encompassing vibration, even the air around me is vibrating in acoustic resonance with the icaro of the maestro.[5]

USING SOUND AND VIBRATION TO SHIFT YOUR ENERGY

Combining vibration, frequency (sound), and intent creates healing. Singing together brings heartbeats into harmony. Combining vocalization and visualization becomes manifestation. The possibilities for working energetically with sound, vibration, and breath to shift your energy are vast. Here are a few possibilities.

CHANTING OM

Chanting OM (AUM), known as the most basic, primal sound, vibrates the heart chakra and shifts you into your heart. According to Hindu belief, when creation began the all-encompassing divine consciousness, or mystical entity, of the universe took the form of OM. This is why you will hear yoga teachers say that OM contains all mantras.[6]

To augment the resonance of these primal sounds, focus on your feelings of compassion and gratitude. Try visualizing pink and gold in your heart, throat, and crown centers as you chant. Combining the energies of sound, feeling, visualization, and intent creates harmony that resonates and radiates outward as far as you intend.

To chant OM, sit with your back straight. Take a deep breath and, from your belly, sound the phonemes AH-OO-MM for as long as you can.

Feel the AH sound resonating in your heart center, the OO sound resonating in your throat center, and the MM sound resonating in your crown center.

Repeat at least three times. And try it in a group, to feel the harmonized energy.

If you enjoy OM, you can expand it to *om mani padme hum,* one of the ancient Sanskrit mantras associated with the bodhisattva of compassion (known as Guanyin, Avalokiteshvara, and Chenrezig).[7]

FINDING YOUR OWN SONGS

Personal songs are a way to explore using vibration for your particular intent, and a way to work with spirit. They do not have to have words or "sound good" to anyone else; personal songs are not performance oriented. You can find songs for releasing, for courage, for drawing in your power, for nonattachment to outcome, and for honoring a place, among other uses.

When you set a strong and clear intent to "find" a song, you can listen as you walk, as you talk to a tree, as you meditate, or as you journey. Once you have a song imprinted in your heart, you may find that it arises to be sung without your conscious thought! This happens, for example, with my song for courage: I will find myself automatically singing it as I drive or am on my way to a challenging meeting. It is as if your body/spirit knows when you need the song before your brain realizes it.

Set your intent to find a song for something specific. Listen carefully. Sing the sounds, tones, words, beat, and rhythms as you receive them. Repeat aloud until your body knows the song. Sing it often, and notice what happens.

USING SOUND TO SHIFT
YOUR ENERGY AND MOOD

There's an easy way to integrate vibration and sound into your energy-shifting tool kit. You can *consciously* identify specific music and songs that help you shift mood, and listen to them.[8] You probably do this already—without thinking about it. That's the intent of many cultural forms of sound—think gospel, flamenco, and blues, for example. Here are some ideas, along with suggestions to get you started.

Identify music or song that:

- Opens your heart (Pachelbel's Canon in D is my favorite)
- Orders and calms your brain so you can focus (Bach's Well-Tempered Clavier works well)
- Makes you want to move with joy (so many choices!)
- Relaxes you
- Drops you into the Theta brain wave state (4 to 7 Hz) for lucid dreaming, visioning, and connecting to the Divine within (rhythmic drumming, rattling, and didgeridoo)
- Helps you remember, in your body, a wonderful and nourishing time in your life (lullabies you sang or that were sung to you)

SILENCE

Entering into silence, or creating the space for it to enter you, is at the root of meditation practices. Entering into silence helps you *be* rather than *do*; instead of distracting yourself with things, exercise, or work, for example, you find a way to rest in what is. It gives you loose, unstructured time to experience whatever is. Quiet leads to attentiveness. Attentiveness creates relaxation. Relaxation makes for improved cognition.[9] Silence makes space for creativity.

As Américo Yábar explains,

One form of meditation is listening to the silence. When you listen to the profound silence of the stone or the voice of the tree you are hearing the voice of the spirit. When you finally hear the silence you will find out that your heart is an instrument of music ... and the silence of the night of time makes it possible for the spirit to come to you and make this instrument play.[10]

CREATING SILENCE

Creating silence is simple. Try this:

Lie in the spring grass looking up at the sky, or put your back next to a tree for ten minutes, really feeling the energy around you. As you become fully present to the sparrow hopping nearby, or the pattern of green leaves on blue sky, you will experience an opening up, a spaciousness. Your worries will drop away, even if only for these ten minutes.

Daydreaming gives your brain and body space to sort through your experience and reach new understanding; silence creates the container in which that can happen.

MEDITATION

Every spiritual and contemplative practice includes some form of meditation to develop tranquility in the depths of your soul. The only way to understand meditation is to do it, just as the only way to love is to do it.

Conscious breathing, awareness, and observation are key. Whether you practice sitting, moving, walking, or visualizing meditations, you develop your experiential perception, what Fritjof Capra calls an "immediate, non-conceptual awareness of reality."

One of the aims of meditation is to silence the thinking mind. Some describe it as a process of interrupting or tricking the mind away from its constant chatter and conceptual framing ("I have to buy milk ... she is mean to me ... this meeting is boring ..."). In meditation, you shift awareness to an intuitive mode of consciousness, and from conceptual to perceptual awareness.

Meditation is central to calming your nervous system and your mind. You can think of meditation as a self-regulating practice that mediates and connects body and brain. "If you are truly focused and paying attention in meditation, your thought will literally become your experience, and your body changes," explains neuroscientist Dr. Joe Dispenza:

> *When we are in a state of creation, we lose the personal: we forget about our problems and our identity. The "self" moves to the heart ... The moment you feel—forgive someone for example—your body feels different. When we can replicate that experience at will, we are in a state of being. The body knows as well as the brain.*[11]

Think of meditation as leading to tranquility in the depths of your soul. Any practice that distracts your thoughts, allows you to rest in your being, and takes your focus out of mind and into breath and silence will help you get there. Any meditation practice—including sitting, breathing, visualization, and movement meditations (like Sufi dancing or qi gong)—helps you develop the skills of concentration, observation, focus, stillness, mindfulness (being present in the moment), and awareness. Meditation in a group enhances the field of energy that supports and sustains personal practice and shared intent. The only way to understand meditation is to do it, just as only way to love is to do it. As Leslie Bryan writes,

> *When you go deeply within and experience stillness and inner peace, your perception will change, your life and the world around you will change. This shift in perception will ripple throughout the entire web of life. Do this for yourself and for all of life on this great earth.*[12]

MOVEMENT

As is true of meditation, sound, and vibration, there are myriad ways of using movement to shift energy. We all move and dance. The difference is that moving and dancing with intent to release, or with intent to fill, changes what happens, and gives you more control over your own energy.

Ancient movement practices like yoga, qi gong, and t'ai chi integrate breath, concentration, and internal awareness with specific positions and movements designed to balance both body and spirit.

More modern movement practices such as Continuum, 5Rhythms, Authentic Movement, Feldenkrais, or Soul Motion add muscle and core awareness to the mix. The body is seen as an instrument of spiritual practice. Danielle Prohom Olson explains,

> *In yogic philosophy all matter contains a spark of divine light, and yoga is about fanning this spark into a flame. The ancient yogis knew spirit energy as the power of life itself and viewed yoga as a form of active communion with that power. As B. K. S. Iyengar put it, "The needs of the body are the needs of the divine spirit which lives through the body.*[13]

Now that you are more familiar with the power of harmonic vibrations to shift your energy, I invite you to step into the deepening that comes with practice. The next chapter will motivate you with the transformative rationale for choosing specific practices and sticking with them! By the end of the chapter you will have the power to change your habits, open your heart, and create a map of consciousness for energy shifting.

Chapter 11
Practice and Transformation

Practice and repetition embed transformation in your body, spirit, psyche, and habits.

You know that to learn how to ride a bike you need to practice; that's how your body remembers. Practice and repetition seem obvious. So what keeps you from practicing?

One problem you may have is that you find excuses, settle into habits, and fail to maintain your energy-shifting, contemplative, or spiritual practice. Another problem you may have is a tendency to take workshop after workshop, or buy book after book, trying to discover something new and better and failing to spend time practicing and integrating what you have already learned. Transformation is challenging!

The practice and the repetition are what count, whether you are using a form of breathing or movement to change energy, a mantra to shift mind focus, or a visualization to open your heart. To paraphrase what Mahatma Gandhi said more than a hundred years ago, "An ounce of practice is worth twenty thousand tons of big talk."[1]

The particular *form* of practice you choose is not important. What is important is that it works for you, gives you pleasure, calms you, and helps you experience change.

Any practice has to fit your specific rhythms and lifestyle. For example, I have found that committing to a regular meditation group works better than promising myself I'll meditate on my own. So learning what works for you is crucial.

When you learn a practice well—doing it repeatedly, making it a habit—you will find it far easier to call upon and implement that practice in times of stress, such as when you are confronted with an emotional challenge. If you have practiced releasing heavy energy and filling with something lighter, you will be more likely to remember to use that practice than to return to an old habit, like eating a bag of potato chips to make yourself feel better.

Four Qualities for Your Transformational Practice

There are many gateways or portals to personal transformation. What makes the exceptional experience—the epiphany, peak experience, or "Aha!" moment—become transformational? Interested in exploring catalysts for and barriers to the way people change, researchers at the Institute for Noetic Sciences spent a decade interviewing spiritual teachers about transformation. In *The Art and Science of Transformation in Everyday Life*, the authors identify four *qualities* a practice needs to have to help you transform:[2]

1. *Intent.* Choosing to make a practice positive for yourself, committing your whole body-mind-spirit, and honoring your limits help feed your transformation.

2. *Attention.* Being mindful of what you perceive, where you are looking and focusing (what works, what does not), and what you talk about replaces your tendency to repeat dysfunctional behavior and negative stories.

3. *Repetition.* Your repetition of a practice helps you transform behavior and recondition your body and mind. You are capable of laying down new neural pathways, no matter what your age.

4. *Guidance.* You need help; you can't do it alone! Either a teacher or noetic/direct understanding—such as you get from practicing energy shifting—can give you the support you need. Surrender to guidance, and the capacity to hold paradox, are also essential.

Every time you engage one of these four qualities, you make a brief, small shift in habit. You expose your body, brain, senses, and heart to a different way of perceiving; you give them respite from what have often become burdensome thoughts; and you reassure them that it is okay to change. As Nicholas Carr writes in *The Shallows*, "... the more times an experience is repeated, the longer the memory of that experience lasts."[3]

In offering you so many varieties of practice for moving and shifting your energy, my intent is to help you embed them in your experiential memory and draw on them whenever you need to. As David Spangler says,

> ... it's the practice, over and over and over—co-creating Grail Space, holding, blessing, honoring, respecting, loving whatever is in my environment and thus connecting myself to the living energy around me— that turns all this into a kind of mental muscle memory ... Practice is learning to amplify a helpful voice. [4]

Moreover, when your body/mind knows how to engage that "helpful voice," you can engage and apply it far more easily in stressful or painful situations.

Setting yourself on a path of moving and shifting your energy can be both a difficult and rich experience. By incorporating intent, attention, repetition, and guidance in your process, you can make your practices more effective and your transformations deeper.

Morning Rhythms: Starting the Day Full and Connected

The first light of the day is known as the "hour of power" in the Andes and elsewhere. It is a fruitful time for insight, focus, and shifting from dream rhythms into waking.

When you honor this time, wonderful images related to your intent, or clarifying phrases related to a project, may come to consciousness just as you wake. For example, I heard "Light helps us regenerate our bodies, like lizards" one morning during the writing of this book. It may sound nonsensical, yet it has had profound meaning for me. Another time, a thought arose that our bodies can be lightning rods and rivers, receiving and transmitting gratitude to the earth.

Creating a morning time of power and focus for yourself is akin to what Barbara Marx Hubbard calls the "Inner Sanctuary," a place of emergence into essence. Suggestions for activities to enhance your focus and connection first thing in the morning (or at any other time that works for you) follow.

WORKING WITH IMAGES

Images from dreams, journeys, and meditation are extremely potent when you wake. Much of your transformation and your ability to connect in new ways comes from nonverbal, experiential perceptions—what some people call "raising vibration" or "entering new dimensions." It's very important to learn to embody the images you are given—that come to you—as you transition with our changing planet.

For example, an image of "stepping into the fire of wisdom" became important to me. For a while, during each morning meditation I reexperienced entering the fire and becoming gold light as a way of exploring and deepening both metaphorical and practical impacts of the image. I experienced sensations of light and fire in my body, and kept observing what was transforming and floating away as ash.

Words for what an image "means" are not important; rather, focus on your embodied experience:

Choose one image from a dream, journey, or meditation and let your body feel into it deeply. Fully experience it before you rise. Repeat daily for as long as the image is potent.

SWALLOWING THE SUN

This practice helps you begin your day as a being of light, connected with the sun itself and with the rhythm of the day. Do this at sunrise to take the light and power of the sun into your body and all your cells:

Facing the sun, tip your head back and open your mouth so the sun hits the roof of your mouth. Swallow the sunlight four times, feeling and seeing the light and heat spreading through your whole torso and into all of your cells.

You do not have to be outside to swallow the sun. If you can see the rising sun from indoors, let the light come through the window and into your mouth.

GIVING YOURSELF A BREAK: STRETCHING AND MEDITATING IN BED

Because my mind is quiet when I wake, I do stretching exercises in bed before I get up. This allows total focus on the muscles and core work. It also guarantees that I will do the stretching; whenever I think, *Oh, I'll do them later*, I never follow through.

I also meditate in bed before rising. The connections I have woken with—dreams, images, and the nature of the day—feed and strengthen my meditation. This is when I consciously experience gratitude and send blessings to suffering places and beings, students, and family. This is when I connect with the web of life and the heart-fields of other light workers. This is one of the times I use energy-shifting practices such as the "The Elements Meditation" (page 93) or "Meditation with the Earth and the Cosmos: Heart Alignment" (page 113).

HAVING A SAY IN YOUR DAY

This practice, from teacher Sarah Dole, starts your morning with connecting and visualizing good results. As you emerge from sleep,

Smile, and express your gratitude for "this most amazing day" (e.e. cummings).

Call in your bright, shining self. Connect with at least one good quality you have.

Thank your guardians, whomever they may be—angels, power animals, saints, tree spirits, fairies—for loving, supporting, and protecting you.

Really feel these connections. From this place of support, scan through the day ahead, seeing each situation in a positive way: The morning goes smoothly. Work is harmonious and productive. Personal interactions are friendly. You are supported in any challenge, whether doctor's appointment or visit with your mother. You are calm and present.

Smile and say, "Thank you!" Your day is off to a great start.

STAYING FOCUSED AND BALANCED WITH YOUR DAILY PRACTICES

I have noticed a common pattern. You find a new practice—breath, exercise, chanting, or meditation—and do it for a while. Then you forget about it, usually in about two weeks! Why is this?

It seems that part of our humanness is to do things because someone says they will be good for us. We are trained to think this way by parents, teachers, and bosses. We have forgotten to determine what we truly want, so we get distracted from the practice. And we procrastinate.

To maintain focus and stop procrastinating, it helps to figure out what really works for you.

My daily practices must meet the five requirements that follow, or I will stop doing them. I also know that if something takes too much time, is too complicated to learn, or stresses rather than calms me, I will stop doing it.

Ask yourself whether your practices:

- Calm and quiet you
- Bring you pleasure
- Help you shift your energy and feel balanced

- Affect both your body and spirit
- Help you feel openhearted, luminous, and connected

Another key way of getting into focus and balance has to do, really, with paying attention. Anytime you are sitting too long, or are thrown off balance by a conversation, or feel stuck, it's important to find ways to:

- Clear your mind
- Get out of your head and into your heart
- Return to your energy body
- Connect with spirit

A third aspect of staying focused is to *choose only a few practices* to do each day. If you have too many, you'll get overwhelmed. You might try choosing one practice for releasing, connecting, and filling and another to bring your body/mind into silence. The particulars are not as important as the repetition to keep yourself in balance.

Working with just a few practices, you *imprint* them in your mind and on your heart. When you *habituate* to them, you can experience your unfolding and *deepening*. As my student Paul reports,

> *I literally use the tools every day. Every aspect of my moment-to-moment awareness in the world has changed. Things do not trigger me as they once might have done. I see a bigger picture in my perception of situations ... Beyond the tools I have learned, what I see (and others have seen as well) is that I have changed fundamentally, at a deep level ... I feel very fortunate that I finally found the seeds of my new beginnings.*

As I keep repeating, there are many methods for shifting your energy. You have to find your own practices, and find what works. The key is to do something! Five minutes of releasing and filling with the elements. A short, mind-clearing walk. Intense exercise on your lunch break. Yoga fire-breath. Toning or singing as you drive. Lying on the earth and breathing in resonance.

CLEANSING AND RELAXING WITH YOUR BREATH

If you tend to repeatedly feel stressed and anxious during the day, or to get overwhelmed by everything you have to do, shifting your energy this way will help you cleanse, relax, and perceive differently.

Like *Savasana*, the yogic relaxation practice, you can use this practice to clear, refresh, and relax your nervous system at any time of day:

> Lying on your back, legs stretched long and arms at your sides, breathe deeply. Feel your breath rise from your lungs to your crown, flow through your whole body, and down to your feet. Then reverse, so the flow moves from your feet all the way through you, cleansing and relaxing you.

DAILY GROUNDING AND PROTECTION: THREE ESSENTIALS

Consciously connecting with the earth (grounding), setting a protective shield, and releasing any psychic hooks others have attached to you are three essentials for your daily energy work. Your intent with these practices—to be connected, and to take in what is appropriate for you and keep out what is not—helps you move through the world in a cleaner and more conscious way. Eighty percent of my clients do not know how to ground and protect; if you are like them, it's time to learn how!

GROUNDING

Use any of the several ways you have already learned for grounding in chapter 4: "Growing Your Roots" (page 71), "Touching Earth" (page 72), or "Being Earth" (page 72).

SETTING PROTECTION

If you are not paying attention to your own energy and the energetic fields around you, you are usually walking around energetically unprotected. This means that, especially if you are sensitive and empathic, you are unconsciously taking in, or taking on, other people's heaviness—their sadness, rage, depression, and so on. To receive only what's appropriate for you and not take in anything that doesn't belong to you (like someone else's anger projection or sadness), you can use a powerful practice from the Chumash people of central and southern California:

> Visualize a blue light around your whole body. See it filling your energy field top to bottom, front to back. Feel the membrane protecting you, yet not keeping out any love or connection that you want to receive. Notice how far the light extends from your physical body, and how big your aura is today.
>
> Say, "I intend to keep out everything that does not belong to me, and let in only what does belong to me."

In this way, you set your intent to allow people's appreciation or love for you, but keep out the anger or frustration that is theirs, not yours. Setting this protection does not keep out the pain of the world, or the pain in your own life. Rather, it helps protect you from energetic invasions that drain your strength.

RELEASING PSYCHIC HOOKS

All of us can hook into other people unconsciously—when we want something from them, when we envy a quality they have that we don't, when we feel needy, or when we are afraid they will leave us. A "psychic hook" is, essentially, an unwanted psychic or emotional connection. It does not help either person, but acts as a kind of invisible burden on the relationship.

When you scan for and release psychic hooks, you are disconnecting from what is not yours and releasing the hook into the universe. It is important to release from yourself, but *not* send the energy back to the person it came from. There need be no judgment or blame involved. Just as when you are working with other kinds of energy, you are not naming it, just letting it go.

> At least once a day, close your eyes and scan your body for anything that feels like a hook. Unhook it. See it rolling away on a cord, rolling through a door. Shut the door. See a rose on the doorknob if you want to, indicating that you mean no harm: you are simply releasing what does not belong to you.

WORKING WITH DISTRACTIONS, KNOWING, AND BEING

Another aspect of daily practice and transformation has to do with what you really need to *know*–the stuff of the mind, information, and data—and what you need to *be*—the focus of the heart.

Our cultural trance is pervasive: we are in a constant state of information overload. Hundreds of social media updates, videos, and blogs come into our computers and mobile devices daily. Governments, the stock market, NGOs, universities, and businesses pour out reports, analysis, data, and more data. Unfortunately, as Nicholas Carr writes, "we become, neurologically, what we think."

There's a strange polarization emerging. You may be an information and analysis junkie. Or you may be an ostrich, metaphorically hiding your head in the sand by avoiding "news," social media, or "facts" as much as possible. For the politically active, burnout and discouragement feed avoidance.

Curiosity is wonderful, but one thing leads to another. We've all had the experience of falling into a pit of online shopping, Twitter posts, gaming, or YouTube videos before we discover that hours have gone by.

QUESTIONS TO ASK YOURSELF

When your intent is clear, you can make choices more easily. Here are questions to ask, every day, to control information distraction so you can focus on making choices about what you need to know:

- Do I need this information for any reason?
- How will this information or activity help me on my life path? Help me stay in balance? Help me stay focused, or not?
- How will this information feed me? (Feeding might be entertaining, fear engendering, distracting, energy shifting, or overwhelming; knowing your intent helps you choose what to feed.)
- What else might I be doing right now?
- In this moment, will I feel happier if I stick with my intent—or cut loose?
- Do I need to do this right now (in the middle of a class or being with my family) or can it wait till I have space to explore new stuff?

Changing a Habit

Your habits can become distractions and serve as excuses. Becoming conscious of them helps you shift from mindless repetition to intentional focus.

The most practical method for changing a habit/distraction is to choose just one that you want to change: your cell phone use, trauma-drama stories, information collection, list making, social media posts, or whatever you feel you do too much of. Then focus on just that one habit. Try to find different ways of doing things that will shake up the habit, and be a little silly as well.

Here's what I mean. Let's say you think you spend too much time on the computer at home. Try opening your computer while you are brushing your teeth, and scan your email only while you brush. This is time limited, goofy, and forces you to stop or you'll drool on the keyboard!

Your intent underlies and feeds everything: reflecting on intent guides what you do, and don't do, during the day. When you know your intent, you can figure out what practices and habits will serve it. The rhythms that take you back into balance will follow. What's important is to pay attention to what works for you, and do it! My friend and poet Sandy Scull writes, in "Against the Talons of Winter Blues,"

> ... *When habit no longer distracts, we begin to sense*
> *the rhythm of things. Like a song rooting*
> *into the earth, patient that one day*
> *it will break ground and enchant the light ...*[5]

Overload and Openheartedness

Having an open heart—knowing what is happening, facing it with equanimity, and paying attention to what you can and cannot attend to—is a viable and rewarding way of being in the world.

Having an open heart helps with your intent, with balance, and with focus: you may no longer need the details of the latest invasion or famine; instead, you may hold those people and places in your heart. In these times of great change, repairing and strengthening the web of interconnections that holds us together may be the essential intent.

Feeding your open heart with the beauty of a creek or the calm of the ocean helps keep it open. Silence helps. Shifting perception and releasing energy help. Having intent and sticking with it help. Being connected with all beings helps you move from overload to open-heartedness.

RELEASING GRIEF OR FEAR

Releasing the energy of your grief or fear—or some other reactive emotion—has a quite amazing effect. The heaviness diminishes or disappears entirely, while the awareness that produced the emotional response remains. Whether you are reacting to terrorism, polar bear habitat loss, or water contamination from fracking, the result is the same: when you release the grief or fear, you heart feels lighter *and* your actions in response come from equanimity and Big Mind, rather that from rage.

> Choose one word that describes your negative emotional response to a situation. Repeating that word, practice "Eating Heavy Energy" (page 60) until your heart feels clear and open.

CREATING YOUR MAP OF CONSCIOUSNESS FOR ENERGY SHIFTING

You are far enough along in exploring energy-shifting practices now to make what I call a map of consciousness for yourself: a guide and reminder of the essentials along your road to transformation. This map will help you integrate principles of energy shifting, practices you want to follow, and your intent for transformation. Doing this, you can make changes you may not believe are possible.

In your map, include:

- Steps you take daily to change your energy, including physical, energetic, and spiritual practices.

  For example, your daily practice might use the pattern of release-connect-fill-open to release the heavy (worries, fear, or pain); "cancel" thoughts of doubt, fear, or judgment; and take in lighter, more inspiring thoughts, energies, and focus.

- How you work with words, vibration, sound, movement, breath, and visualization to work with your energy.

  For example, you might intend to feed your health and joy (not your illness or problems) with your words, the stories you tell, and your attitude. You might focus on replacing thoughts of "fighting" an illness with a more cooperative, reciprocal focus. You might choose to listen to the messages your body gives you.

- How you engage with the living beings surrounding you—both human and nonhuman—to increase your sense of support.

  For example, you might look for support from a pet, a tree, or a friend. You might retrain yourself to receive support you are offered, and remember it on your challenging days. You might find a nourishing "place" for yourself and your spirit, a parallel world you can visit any time.

- Reminders to yourself.

  For example, you might remind yourself: "I have power. I have the power of intent, of focus, of connection, and of seeking wholeness." You might focus on trusting your internal authority, and listening to your heart, asking, "Tell me what I need to know."

In essence, when your map of consciousness follows the basic energy-shifting pattern of releasing and filling, you are well on your way. Your embodied experience will guide you into your heart and the heart of the universe. As Deepak Chopra advises:

Be the shift inside you, then you can communicate the shift and hang out with the people who are resonating at the same frequency. In the end, things do evolve because that's the nature of consciousness—it struggles, it experiments, it fails, and it takes creative leaps ... The result over time is that the advantages to those living in a unified field naturally emerge.[6]

With a clear sense of how your practice embeds transformation in your body, spirit, psyche and habits, you are ready to dive deeper into the four pillars of perception in the upcoming chapters. In chapter 12, I invite you to discover the full meaning of intent. You will learn the power of your intent to create change and affect both personal and global outcomes, and to use decree and love talk as you deepen your sacred journey.

Chapter 12
Intent

Intent includes your energetic attention, passion, spirit, and focus. Intent comes from your essence rather than your thoughts: your third eye gives you the vision to see the whole. Your heart helps you feel your way into action with love, compassion, and intuition. Your power center in your belly helps you live with integrity. Thus intent arises from your whole being, not just your mind and thoughts. This difference is crucial.

Intent does not come from *will*, with which you try to push through no matter what. Intent is different from *desire*, your mind's idea of what will make you happy, what you want, what you wish for. Intent is different from *affirmations*, the practice of positive thinking and repeatedly saying what you want to believe. Intent is also different from *intention*, which is action oriented and goal directed in English usage.

True intent includes the whole—your body, mind, heart, and spirit, the light and the heavy, sunlight and shadow. True intent takes into account your weaknesses as well as your strengths, so it doesn't set you up to fail. As Wayne Dyer says, intent is not dogged determination but an inner awareness "that exists in the universe as an invisible force of energy."[1]

It took me a long time to understand intent. I was so steeped in the dominant paradigm of using will—deciding to do something and *making* it happen—that I learned slowly what it meant to ease into something that was important to me. When I wrote technical books for Silicon Valley companies, the whole team—engineers, product designers, writers, marketers—worked under artificial deadlines defined by someone's idea of when a product should come to market. We had to produce according to schedule, to make our parts happen.

When I wrote this book with intent, in contrast, it did not work to make schedules, timelines, or set goals; I had to learn to flow with the wisdom as it arose.

If you have the intent now to be connected with the living energy around you, how would that look? When the winter sun shines low through your window, will you turn to it and take in its warmth, swallow its light? When you wake in the night with worry, will you shift your attention by breathing it out into the elements and breathing in the energy of fire, water, earth, and air? Will you flow with your need to step outside the box of your electronic devices and stop to exchange energy with a tree?

Moving with intent sends an energetic vibration into the world. It affects your cells, your fields, and the web of life that surrounds you. It feeds what you are trying to create—whether personally or globally—and affects the cumulative outcome of your choices. Developing your intent helps you change your perception and experience of the problems in your life. It is one of the four pillars of perception—those qualities that help you shift your experience of the world into one of connection and openheartedness.

THE POWER OF INTENT TO CREATE CHANGE

A month after we began working together, a student of mine had a mastectomy. Despite her surgery, despite the obvious loss, and despite the heavy feelings that accompany cancer, Joan appeared radiant. She explained to me that she had been visualizing all the participants in her treatment coming together to support her.

Part of Joan's energetic response—her intent—she said, was to *work with*, not *fight against* the disease in her body. She understood, in her heart, that the energy of fighting simply engenders more fighting; she intended a different stance. This perception alone was a major deviation from our dominant thought patterns and medical models: we have all been trained to think about fighting cancer and disease.

Joan focused her energy on what she called the "highest and best outcome," meaning that she did what she could to heal and entertained the possibility of perfect health while allowing for anything to happen. She was practicing what Buddhists and shamans call nonattachment to outcome. To support this intent, she focused on staying in her energy body, her three centers, as various emotions, fears, and responses of others arose.

She repeated her intent daily before surgery and during chemotherapy, radiation, and recovery. Joan visualized the surgical team, the hospital staff, the machines, and her body working together cooperatively. She visualized herself healed, strong, and well. Joan paid attention to the thoughts, attitudes, stories, and habits that had resulted in her physical imbalances, working to transform them as she discovered them. We all know this takes time and courage. She engaged with her community for support, making sure to spend time with those who understood her intent. She stepped aside, as much as possible, from those who responded by feeding fear and anxiety in their words and energetic responses. When people said, "Oh, how terrible," Joan felt it triggered her fear and did not help her stay aligned with her intent.

But Joan didn't depend on just vision and words. By staying in alignment in her three centers, by releasing and filling energetically, and by keeping her centers of power, loving action, and vision focused and light filled as much as possible, she moved with integrity. She modeled for me, and everyone who knew her, the power of intent to create change. By moving the heavy energy through and out, she repeatedly released the idea that curing her cancer was the only acceptable result.[2]

DEVELOPING YOUR INTENT

You have been working with intent all along as you've explored practices for changing your energy. The focus of this chapter is to help you change your perceptions of relationships, responsibilities, and "reality" itself as you deepen your understanding and use of intent.

Your perception of what's possible is essential in forming your intent. When you do not believe something is possible, you can't experience or envision it: you are stuck with what you know and think is true.

Honing your intent comes from your experience, and each change in your experience helps you take the next step, and then the next.

When setting your intent, draw on your whole being: your vision, compassion, power, and reciprocity. This helps you step into sacred time, what Alberto Villoldo calls the "stream of infinity," a place of pure potential.

By offering your intent to the universe, by asking for the help of all living beings, and by releasing any attachment to particular outcomes, you set in motion an unfolding of possibilities. Flowing in this river of possibilities, and feeding your intent with practice, ceremony, alignment, and awareness, you move into the dreaming.

How Setting Intent Feeds Change

Setting your intent to heal a physical injury is a good example of how intent feeds change. When you believe you can heal, you are motivated to exercise. When doing your exercises results in less pain and more strength, you keep doing them. When you feel your body become stronger and less stiff, that fuels your intent to keep up the exercise! When you stop, as we all do, and the pain returns, you have some choices: You can renew your intent. You can give up. You can try something different. You can make excuses. You can feed your fear of being disabled. You can vow to do the best you can.

Setting your intent to have an open heart in a difficult relationship is another example. If you remind yourself daily that you want to keep your heart open and your interactions with the person become easier, you are likely to continue. If you identify some limiting thoughts and release them, you are more likely to be able to stay in your open heart. When you keep yourself in alignment, you get better at remaining openhearted and being confident in your intent.

Setting your intent does not mean you can control the outcome. You are simply doing the best you can to shift your part in a situation or interaction, and to feed a different energy.

In fact, nonattachment to outcomes helps make your intent cleaner; if you get mad because you didn't get what you intended, you have created more heavy energy for yourself!

For example, the other person in a difficult relationship may refuse to forgive, seem oblivious to your openheartedness, or hold on to their version of events, their story. If you blame them in return, you have lost your openheartedness. Instead of blaming, you might consider how you can let go of your reactivity and protect yourself from more hurt. You might ask yourself what you need in order to stay openhearted. In this process of reconsidering your intent, you will certainly find clarity and learn a lot.

Magnetizing Support for Your Intent

Setting intent means creating a fluid membrane in your energy field so something different can enter. Setting your intent and acting on it are ways of magnetizing support from and connection with others who share your focus. Setting intent is a way to open the portals more clearly to your own path in life.

Your intent colors, drives, and fuels everything. Your intent impacts the larger field just as scientists have learned: the moment intent is framed, action begins; there is no time lapse. And just as others are affected by your intent, you are affected by theirs.

Think about the practice of gratitude. Over the last decade there has been a collective effort to help people learn gratitude, practice gratitude, and be inspired by expressions of gratitude. As the practice spread, friends talked and emailed each other, set up social media pages, encouraged each other. People thought of fun ways, like the "Free Hugs" viral movement, of being in gratitude. Knowing others shared the intent to live in gratitude helped each person maintain her commitment. Feeling the effects around the world encouraged the intent. The same thing can happen in your family, your workplace, and the groups you engage with.

Intent, Creation, and Decree

Your words and thoughts, and the intent they express, carry energy, so it is important to notice *how* you express what you are trying to manifest. What you observe can help you identify any hesitations you have. Only when you discover that you are putting limitations on the outcome can you address those limitations.

We've let others—parents, corporations, media, and government—define the world for us. Our cultural narratives are primarily stories of conflict and competition, winners and losers. What happens when you stop complaining about what is wrong and try to imagine the world you'd like to live in? You often discover, to your surprise, how hard it is to be specific in your vision. You might imagine world peace, but have trouble describing what that would look like. You might envision a great relationship, but be challenged to describe how your life would feel different.

Using all your senses—sound, smell, taste, touch, and hearing—helps you create a vivid picture. Seeing and feeling yourself in the world you imagine helps you focus your intent.

Expressing intent as a *decree* is a way to engage your power, your heart perception, and your internal authority. A decree helps you experience the world you are creating. Feeling it makes it more tangible; saying it feeds a different world and dreams it into being. Imagining and believing you are connected in the field of the loving universe create a vibration that supports your decrees.

FRAMING INTENT AS DECREE

Here are some examples of decrees you can use to create your own:

> I see myself in a fulfilling, sustainable, stimulating job.
> I create a world where the breath of spirit flows from heart to heart.
> I see my family (self, partner, child) healthy, strong, energized, whole, and joyful.
> I create a world where everyone perceives the living energy in all things.

It's good to fill in the details as you make heartfelt decrees. For example, if your intent is to be healthy, you might say with every meal, and every time you exercise,

> I feed my health, balance, and energy. I intend to strengthen muscles and release pain. I forgive myself everything I cannot do, and did not do.

If your intent is to lessen stress, you might remind yourself,

> Worry causes heaviness. I see myself relaxed, light, and radiant.

If your intent is to support a friend struggling with sorrow, you might say (and believe),

> I see you finding your way with joy. I see you moving through this time like a river. I see you shedding every fear and anxiety so you can be fully present in each moment.

Your intent is to express compassion for the friend's suffering. Your intent is also to avoid repeating and feeding that suffering, loss, depression, and so on in your conversations, as you might if you said, "Oh that is so awful. I feel so bad for you."

The more you envision your intent, the more possible it becomes! The more you act on your intent, the stronger it becomes.

MORE KEYS TO DEVELOPING YOUR INTENT

Your intent can focus on anything from a daily way of being in the world to a major life change. It's important to engage your three centers—power in your belly, love in your heart, and wisdom in your third eye—as you form your intent.

Forming intent is a spiraling path where each insightful step leads to the next in a non-linear process. You may need to be receptive, silent, open, patient, and trusting. You will need to pay attention to your attachment to outcome, and adjust your intent accordingly. You must be willing to remove obstacles of belief and find other ways of perceiving. You always have choices.

It is useful to think of creating a map of consciousness, a route you can follow along the path where your intent takes you. Think of the map as a guide to changing the message for your energetic, spiritual, and physical selves, your whole field. Think of the map as the steps you can take to release what no longer serves, and find practices to feed your intent day by day. Think of the map as a guide for experiencing your shifts.

ASKING USEFUL QUESTIONS

Here are some questions to ask, listening to your belly, heart, and mind as you answer yourself and frame your intent:

- What is my vision? How can I experience that vision with all my senses?
- How does my heart's wisdom feed this intent?

- What energetic stance do I want to take? What attitudes can I bring to this process?
- How can I experience my path as a spiral, rather than as a straight line?
- Who are my allies (friends, skills, beliefs, habits, personal strengths)? Who among my family and friends will not support me very well in this intent?
- How will I act on and demonstrate my commitment to my intent? What daily practices will help me?
- How do I want to talk about my intent (or not)?
- What kind of response from others would help me?
- Are any of my old issues, stories, or habits going to get in the way? Am I willing to move some boulders, or let go of something, to follow though? What changes in lifestyle am I willing to make (or not)?

STATING YOUR WHOLE INTENT

Stating the whole of your intent as a decree ("this is what I see") rather than a plea ("please help me") is empowering. You can modify these words to fit your specific intent:

I see an easy surgery, filled with light, love, and long-term healing. I intend that all the tools use their highest intelligence for physical illumination and energetic healing. I intend a quick release of all toxins, energetic and physical, from drugs and anesthesia in my body.

I see my healing as smooth, quick, and requiring minimal pain medication. I see a full reunion of body, soul, and spirit post-surgery.

I intend that my recovery will be easy, radiant, empowering, and fast. I see my reconfigured body luminous in every cell, strong and healthy beyond my wildest dreams. I see the reunion of body and spirit ongoing, deepening, and shining into the world.

YOUR EXPECTATIONS, STORIES, AND ENERGY

Your expectations, beliefs, and ideas about what is possible play a major role in outcome. You create the reality you expect to see.

Studies on both placebo and "nocebo" effects, for example, repeatedly show that your expectations about whether you will stay sick or get well determine the outcome. These expectations are so strong that they override treatments. As Deepak Chopra writes, "... the body can turn any mental intent into its chemical correlation."[3]

As I have mentioned before, our stories, memories, cultural assumptions, and embedded emotions can get in the way of the best intent. Your intent can push up against your habits, both personal and cultural. For example, a habit of overcommitment may make following through with a new project a challenge. A habit of avoidance can get in the way of doing something you say you intend to do. If you do not believe you are good enough, your intent to get a better job or find a mate will be sabotaged by underlying emotions.

This is why practices to shift energy are so essential: *They teach your body new ways of being.* They help you replace the stories, emotions, and assumptions that no longer serve you. They make space for shifting into "lighter" feelings that connect you to the world in different ways.

Making space for the new always involves releasing the old, transforming, and transmuting.

PRACTICING LOVE TALK

In the Celtic tradition, the ancient Irish practice of "love talk" gives you a way to think about incorporating expectation, possibility, and the whole in setting intent.[4] Notice how each love talk embraces dichotomy and shadow as well as possibility.

Beautiful the steep mountain pass,
Beautiful too these sore muscles walking.

Beautiful these barren branches,
Beautiful too the spring they portend.

Beautiful life's joys and sorrows.
Beautiful too this moment of peace.

Beautiful the foggy morning,
Beautiful too the sun burning through.

YOUR SACRED JOURNEY

It is with intent that you create meaning and effect change. Working with your intent has all the potential of a sacred journey: seizing an opening, entering, choosing the way to move, finding meaning along the path, overcoming obstacles, and changing as result of the journey.

The earliest story ever written, in Sumer, tells of such a sacred journey. Inanna, the Sumerian Queen of Heaven and Earth, must shed all her garments—symbols of her power—as she passes through seven gates to reach the underworld.[5] She arrives with only her naked intent, the clear sense of purpose that guides and sustains her actions and emotions. When she returns from the underworld, she uses the power of her intent to continue on her path, despite the personal cost, loss, and changes she has incurred.

WEAVING A WEB OF LIGHT AT THE FULL MOON

At each full moon, join your intent with others around the world to create and energize a human web of light, spreading and shining around the earth.[6] You can teach and share this with children; you can weave the web alone or with a group.

We humans are light embodied. We draw on this light, our essence, to shine brightly and weave our web of light within and throughout the earth on the full moon. We create a circle of connection and radiance for anyone who needs it to draw upon.

> On the night of the full moon, find a quiet place where you can see the moon.
>
> Go inside yourself, finding your stillness, your essence, your light. Feel it shine inside. Absorb it into all your cells. Experience it radiating out from you.
>
> Let yourself experience union with the light of the moon and the power of the universe. Keep focusing on your light, and your intent to shine.
>
> Let yourself sink into connection with all the other lights. See the web of light weaving with moonlight, glowing and growing until it circles the earth.
>
> Rest in this light, letting it fill every cell.

THE MYSTERY OF INTENT

When you explore your intent, possibilities and hope abound. Your sensations and perceptions arise and fall away moment by moment. In a state of "interbeing"—the emptiness, or a sense of wholeness without boundaries that allows you to feel connected with all living creatures—breath, light, and energy move through you so strongly that cosmic connection is all that is important, and ego dwindles away.[7] In this state, intent becomes a vast, open expanse. Awe takes over, and the portal opens into wondrous, amazing mystery.

Whatever dreams you have—for yourself, and for the world—will become reality. This is the nature of the holographic universe! To dream brave, light-filled dreams means you must release your limiting beliefs, push past your fears, and set your intent.

In this chapter you have gained a grounded sense of how to apply intent to your practice of shifting energy and making changes in your life. Now I invite you to discover the power of alignment, another pillar of perceptual change. In chapter 13 you will learn to align yourself to feel centered, fluid, and in resonance. You will see how alignment helps you build the muscle of your relationship with living energy, step away from dissonance, and enter more resonant vibrational states. You will experience the implications of aligning your breath, your three centers, and your consciousness in resonance.

Chapter 13
Alignment and Resonance

When you align yourself, you are reorganizing, adjusting, and lining up all your parts so you can become resonant, internally and externally. Such resonance is a form of renewal and, like intent, is a pillar of perceptual change. Developing alignment and resonance helps you shift the ways in which you experience your relationships, responsibilities, and "reality" itself. Learning to align with the living universe helps you belong.

Energetic alignment helps you feel flow, attunement, and connectedness in your internal sense of the world as well as your relations with others. Just as you get your car tires aligned for better performance and wear, or your bones aligned so your muscles have to do less work, you can align your energy so your interactions can become fluid.

In a dialogue with Matthew Fox, Rupert Sheldrake summarized the importance of alignment and resonance:

> We now think scientifically of all nature as vibratory. Everything is rhythmic, oscillatory, even down to the heart of the atom.... Any response must involve resonance.[1]

Jean Millay, a pioneer in the field of biofeedback, explains how resonance establishes connection: "If you can establish a resonance with something's vibrating energy, you become it."[2]

WHY ALIGN YOURSELF ENERGETICALLY?

You know how it feels to be aligned and centered—or not—within yourself. When you *are* aligned energetically, you experience fluidity, ease, receptivity, connection, and resonance. Smoothness and respect underlie your interactions. Your three centers are lined up: you don't feel conflicts between your power, heart, and vision.

When you are *not* aligned, you experience dissonance and feel stuck. You may experience power struggles with others, or your gut may feel one thing and your heart another. Conversations push your buttons; you may misunderstand or feel misunderstood. This means that your energetic centers of power are disordered; they are not in alignment.

We all experience these effects in our significant relationships. When you are in alignment with a partner, child, or dear friend, things flow, even when you and they are not wanting or doing the same things. When you are in a state of nonalignment, your differences with another person can feel huge, magnified out of proportion to their importance.

Yet the possibilities of energetic alignment are vast. You can align yourself with any living being or energy field in the cosmos! You might want to try aligning with a tree, a sacred place, a work group, an ecosystem, your family, your intent, a group energy field, the earth, the universe, or an animal. These kinds of alignments help you shift from perceiving something as *outside* yourself to experiencing your deep connection and bringing the energy *inside*.

Oscar Miro Quesada explains the ancient human impetus toward alignment:

> *Indigenous culture is based on the understanding that people are not moved through persuasion; rather, people are moved through being aligned in purpose ... one's experience of communion and reconnection with the living earth always arouses the desire to act on its behalf ... (and when) you act on behalf of something greater than yourself, you begin to feel it acting through you with a power that is greater than your own.*[3]

When you are harmonized through alignment, you create a unified field of consciousness, where complementarity becomes more important than separation and disharmony.

SHIFTING YOUR CONSCIOUSNESS THROUGH ALIGNMENT

You've been working with alignment all along as you've explored practices to change your energy. The focus of this chapter is to help you change your perceptions of yourself, your life, and the world around you as you deepen your understanding and your use of alignment.

What you align your power, heart, and wisdom with—moment to moment, day by day, year by year—is essential to your consciousness. It is a huge vehicle for directing your own energy, intent, and action.

Learning to come into energetic alignment teaches you how to step out of heavy energy, conflict, and mental concepts like "The news is bad," "I have too much to do," or "I am so worried." It's a tool you can use to bring yourself back into full presence in the moment and into awareness of all that is.

Learning to come into alignment is one way to build the muscle of your relationship with living energy, your perceptual awareness of both the seen and unseen. It strengthens your ability to engage with the living energy fields of other beings. It is a step on the path toward dropping the veils of separation—focusing on the small self, the ego, the purely personal—and opening to the wider universe and the communal.

Coming into alignment teaches you how to shift into more resonant vibrational and energetic states, internally and externally. It is a way to engage your three centers so you can amplify your capacity to perceive.

Coming into alignment creates resonance and flow between you and the universe. It gives you insight and the courage to keep going, along with the power to stand firm through any change, any disaster. It reorients you to what is alive, vivid, and pulsing in your life. An extraordinary experience I had, a lightning initiation, illustrates the power of cosmic alignment:

When a sudden downpour becomes a deluge, we hike down fast, feeling the trail turn to mush under our feet. Reaching a palapa (a building with a palm-thatch roof and open sides) above the river, exhausted and sopping wet, we light a fire and hover around it, waiting for the storm to end. I stare through sheets of rain at the roiling, muddy, rising river. In my fatigue-altered state, the heat, light, and rain are intense, as if I have entered another dimension, the disintegration my meditation has foretold.[4]

Then lightning strikes, shaking the ground under our feet, illuminating everything. It's very close. Américo tells us to welcome it, to reach up our arms and pull it down with the thunder. Three times we reach up and pull in those electrified moments of brilliant flash and rumble. I complete the motions in a daze, barely able to concentrate on lifting my arms.

In the Andes, they believe that if the first ray of lightning hits near you and doesn't kill you, it breaks your etheric body into pieces and spreads it out. Like my meditation disintegration, I think. The second ray of lightning brings the etheric body back together; the third ray produces ecstatic contemplation and returns you to an incorruptible unity, kaka haypicha. *Rays of jungle lightning, el raio, come from the fire of the cosmos, entering and changing your consciousness of everything.*

Américo says our lightning experience is alchemical, and that the elements are in charge, producing a karpay, *or initiation, putting our group into "the dimension of lightning." The lightning gives us a deeper experience of the interconnectedness of all beings than I have ever known before.*

When the rain lets up and the river calms, we quietly pile into the boat and return to the lodge, each in her own sensory world. I retreat to my room. When I'm called to the bonfire and barbecue our host has prepared, even the remnants of my social graces disintegrate: I refuse to join in. I am outside time, promises, and commitments. No mind, just body, the sound of rain battering the tin roof above my room, and lightning in the night.

The sensory jungle deluge washes away all vestiges of my shields, defenses, and self-protection; my habitual perceptions disintegrate. I experience "the profound silence of the interior light," a heart fullness where everything is in alignment, and my spirit soars. I feel at one with the mystery of the cosmos, without fear.

Developing Your Alignment

Breath, meditation, observation, and energy practices can assist you in coming into alignment.

As with all tools, *practice, integration,* and *using* alignment are what are important. All these practices take you toward a felt sense of *In La'kesh,* the Mayan phrase meaning "I am another yourself."

This is a subtle process, felt through the energy centers in our bellies, hearts, and third eyes rather than with the understanding of mind.

My healer friend Elizabeth describes it this way:

Alignment is an energetic connection without words. As my hands rest on the person's shoulders I let my energy settle and notice where their energy vibrates. I look for the moment when our two tones, our two voices, merge as one. That moment of harmony is when I feel my heart respond, expand, and come into alignment with theirs. When I let my vibration match theirs, there is harmony and I can give healing energy to them. The alignment facilitates the transference of the energy, smoothly, through me to them. The aligning allows a synchronization of our hearts. The energy is transferred at the heart level.[5]

Another healer friend, Moria, explains:

When I intend alignment with another person, and place my hands on that person, I start by expanding my consciousness. I feel this as an expansion at the back of my neck and/or base of my skull out to around my ears. In this expanded state, I send my perception down my arms (or wherever the physical points of contact might be) and sense the tides within the other person's body: the movements of breath, blood, and energy, but especially breath.

I find it incredibly powerful to align my breath with someone else's, usually matching. Once the tides are sensed and the breathing starts to harmonize, alignment comes naturally, like that study [by Bernie Krause] where the trees aligned with meditators sitting next to them. If I couldn't touch the person for whatever reason, I could still align, if the conditions were calm enough, by simply reaching out energetically. I expect that with practice, like meditation, I could align under most external conditions. It's also easier if I know the person, because there's already a bond between us.[6]

What these two healers are describing is a common experience for those who work holistically with both physical and energetic healing. Such alignment is central to shamanic healing as well. When dissimilar energies are aligned and harmonized, the healer and the recipient experience themselves in a unified field where insight and perception flow beyond the boundaries of their individual minds.

Neuroscientists talk about the capacity of "limbic resonance," a "symphony of mutual exchange and internal adaptation whereby two mammals become attuned to each other's inner states."[7] Because your nervous system is not self-contained, but rather demonstrably attuned to those around you—those with whom you share a close connection—you have a great capacity for sharing deep emotional states with others. Empathic harmony, fear, anxiety, and other resonant states arise from the limbic system of the brain. Limbic resonance feeds your capacity to align energetically with others. Your intent feeds your choices about which energies to align with.

BREATHING INTO ALIGNMENT

A simple and wonderful way to align energetically involves breathing together. It's especially useful when you feel out of sorts with a loved one, whether child, partner, or friend. It's a quick and easy way to shift together so that whatever project you're doing—conversation, lovemaking, problem solving—flows seamlessly. The focus of truly paying attention to the other's breathing takes you out of your mental constructs and into the arising and passing of breath, like waves.

It is best done together, yet you can do your breathing part without the other person even noticing (I often align with my husband as we are falling asleep). When centering, calming down, and coming into internal alignment are what's needed, this breath practice works well.

When the other person breathes out, you breathe in. When the other person breathes in, you breathe out, matching your rhythms.

Continue breathing together until your heart slows, your belly calms, your vision expands, and you feel again the deep resonance you have together.

ALIGNING YOUR THREE CAULDRONS

In Celtic cosmology, your three centers are known as your three cauldrons, representing your true self and your soul. In the old days, cauldrons were big pots used for hearth cooking. They could contain, and cook, everything.

The Three Cauldrons is an ancient Celtic practice taught by Tom Cowan. When you align your three cauldrons, you use the image or visualization of a cauldron in your belly, heart, and third eye to focus. Power comes from aligning them. It is a way of getting in touch with your true self, your full essence.

You learned a different version of this practice—"Filling and Aligning Your Three Centers" (page 70)—in chapter 4. Because it is so useful in alignment, I will repeat it here:

> Visualize a cauldron inside your belly. See the cauldron fill with healing gold light, until it is full and spilling over with light.
>
> Visualize the gold light flowing upward from your belly cauldron, filling the cauldron in your heart. See your heart cauldron full and spilling over with light.
>
> See the gold light flowing upward towards the cauldron in your third eye. Feel your third eye cauldron full of light and spilling over, circulating down to the cauldrons in your belly and heart, and up again.
>
> See the light flowing between all three cauldrons until you feel calm, full, and realigned.

You can use this practice to explore filling and aligning your cauldrons with any light (not just gold light), vibration, or other living being.

ALIGNING WITH ANOTHER LIVING BEING

All living beings share the three cauldrons—energetic centers—in belly, heart, and third eye. You can therefore align your cauldrons with those of another being.

This is a wonderful way to learn somatically about the experience and connectedness of other beings. One day after I had been lucky enough to see Coho salmon spawning, I decided to align my three cauldrons with theirs. In my belly cauldron I experienced their calm, wildness, focused intent, and power. In my heart cauldron, as I aligned with salmon's heart cauldron, I became connected with the whole forest and ecosystem, in resonance with all. When I aligned my third eye cauldron with salmon's, my experience was of Gaia consciousness, vast qi, no other. What blessings we can receive in this practice!

Suspending judgment and playfully engaging your imagination are helpful, as the three centers of a tree or a mountain may not feel the same or look like yours. Try this with a tree, a pet, and a place you love so you can explore the individual variations in living beings.

Fill your three cauldrons (see "Aligning Your Three Cauldrons" (page 171)).

Find a tree you like. Ask the tree's permission, politely. Focus on the cauldron in your belly, aligning it with the tree's belly cauldron (it may not feel like yours!).

Repeat with your heart cauldron and the tree's heart cauldron.

Repeat with your third eye cauldron and the tree's third eye cauldron. Notice whether your body or breath change as you align with the tree.

You might also try moonlight, sunlight, rainbow light, and black light. You might align with the vibration of wind, or the Northern Lights, or the sounds of silence, or with love, power, or excitement. You might align with another person, a river, a stone, a power animal, or a flower you love. This is a powerful and quick way to develop your relationship with many kinds of living energy.

ALIGNING TO RELEASE FEELINGS OF SEPARATION FROM ANOTHER

Alignment also helps you get past disharmonious thoughts and feelings of separation from another. I have found this practice useful when I am experiencing some dissonance with a friend, or with the earth herself, especially when I do not understand the cause.

Your intent is central to this practice. It is like trying to forgive someone: sometimes you discover that you are not really ready to forgive, or to come into harmony and alignment. It is important not to judge yourself in this, but simply to acknowledge that this is not the time. On the other hand, when your intent is strong, aligning with another person can help you get beyond the stuck places and see how to resolve the differences.

> Set your intent to come into alignment with the person in question. Align your three cauldrons, as above.

> Now focus on the cauldron in your belly, aligning it with the other person's belly cauldron. Repeat with your heart cauldron and the person's heart cauldron. Repeat with your third eye cauldron and the person's third eye cauldron.

> Notice how your breath and feelings change as you align. If one of the centers/ cauldrons is more difficult to align, pay attention: that may give you clues to the nature of the misalignment between you.

ALIGNING WITH A GROUP

All of us are engaged with many kinds of groups—through work, school, social media, friends, volunteering, common interest, and so on. When you feel out of sync with the rest of the group, you probably take things personally or blame someone else. Yet the energies of conflict often have different sources from what we experience.

Using the practice of alignment to find resonance with a group you are in, or to determine what the imbalances are or where they lie, is a useful, nonlinear way to make your life more fluid and easy.

For example, in a volunteer land preservation group I work with, an event we were planning suddenly became fraught with frustration, blame, and hurt feelings between two of the other members. Using alignment, I was able to see the source of conflict in their different styles of planning, rather than in personalities or competencies. By gently pointing out the differences, I was able to smooth ruffled feathers so we could continue to function in resonance.

> Set your intent to come into alignment with the group. Align your own three cauldrons, as above.

> Align the cauldron in your belly (your power) with the group's belly cauldron. Align your heart cauldron (your love) with the group's heart. Align your third eye cauldron (your insight) with that of the group.

> Pay attention to your feelings and breath in each of the centers, watching for clues to the nature of the misalignment.

ALIGNING WITH THE LIVING ENERGY AROUND YOU

Aligning with the living energy of everything—qi, kawsay, Gaia consciousness—can lead you to unity consciousness, where subject and object become one. Sitting outside in silence is a way of perceiving union that is known the world over.

> Find a place outside to sit quietly and comfortably. Settle into your internal silence, listening and watching with awareness. As you notice and sense the trees, plants, birds, and whatever else surrounds, let yourself rest in this awareness. Let yourself breathe into the world around you.
>
> Breathe out the worries and monkey-mind. Breathe in the energies of all these other beings. Fill yourself. Keep breathing this way until you notice that you have shifted into a larger awareness.
>
> Notice how breathing shifts the energy in your belly, in your heart, and in your third eye. Notice how your perception shifts.

ALIGNING WITHIN SACRED SPACE

Creating "sacred space"—a circle of protection into which you invite helping ancestors, animals, and spirits, the elements, and the six directions to join you for inquiry, ceremony, and healing—is a key way to explore alignment.

While most of us first experience sacred space someone else created at a ceremony or ritual, there is no reason not to learn to create it yourself. The more you learn to engage and work with the inter-being-ness of your world, the more powerful your work becomes.

Creating sacred space involves intent, receptivity, alignment, and reciprocity. You may follow these steps:

- Intent: Ask, who and what beings am I calling in, and why?
- Receptivity: Ask, am I willing to engage with spirit helpers, elementals, and other dimensions? Do I trust that they are present, whether I can "see" them or not, and that they are helping beings?
- Alignment: Ask, as I invite the "unseen" into my space, can I come into resonance, drop my ego (self-importance), and be a "hollow bone" for information to flow through me?

- Reciprocity: Now engage respectfully and honor whomever joins you. For example, you may sing, rattle, dance, and drum, calling other beings to help and support you.

Creating sacred space is a way of focusing, quieting, opening, and reconnecting yourself or a group with the living energies surrounding you. It is best when everyone participates and it is done consistently. It begins the process of coming together as the whole-larger-than-the-parts.

Around the world there are many different ways of creating sacred space before ceremony, healing work, or council. Whether you copy a particular cultural practice or create your own way of calling the sacred, your intent, alignment, reciprocity, and receptivity are key to the power of the calling and the power of the space.

DAILY ALIGNMENT MEDITATIONS

All the ancient movement practices—yoga, t'ai chi, qi gong, and so on—contain elements of alignment. The deeper you go into these spiritual practices, the more alignment possibilities you can discover.

Certain activities are naturally aligning: working with clay or glass, toning, gardening, and walking meditation, for example. In any creative activity, you have to be in resonance with the "material"—as you know if you have ever tried to make a ceramic pot while you are distracted, or have rushed to plant your vegetables. When you focus your full attention on the activity, your internal dialogue dissipates. You become one with what you are doing.

MEDITATING YOURSELF INTO ALIGNMENT

Four other meditations in this book are especially helpful for coming into alignment on a daily basis:

- "The Elements Meditation" (page 93) and "Creating Sacred Space with the Elements Meditation" (page 94), to align with the four elements, your allies, power objects, and spirit helpers.

- "Meditation with the Earth and the Cosmos: Expanding Your Connections" (page 114) , to strengthen and align your connections with the earth, the heavens, and the sacred mountains or places you feel most connected to.
- "Connecting the Dots: Taking a Moment of Love" (page 108) , to expand your sense of loving connection.

Whatever practice of alignment you choose, you will notice that your body relaxes, your heart opens, and your senses enliven. Alignment opens you to the perspective of mystery and the living energy river of love that surrounds and flows through you.

Resonant Implications

Once your skill in aligning, internally and in your relationships with others, is well developed, the possibilities are vast. As David Spangler writes, "a larger relational field can emerge out of any relationship in which there is a smidgeon of connection and caring.[8]

You get better at focusing your energy and attention. Your perceptual framework broadens. Your alignment with others roots you in times of turbulence. Every practice that connects you with more refined energy (that of alignment rather than that of separation, for example) becomes a vehicle for both protection and transformation. You can use your alignment to create stronger resonance in groups and energy fields, shifting the connection, process, and engagement within the whole field. Truly, in resonance there is no "other."

An example of this is found in hunter-gatherer societies that seek to join with the natural world and use its powers. Elizabeth Marshall Thomas writes,

> The Ju/wasi ... would feel the change in the air, notice the behavior of the clouds that built in the western sky, know that rain was coming, and make themselves ready to join with the oncoming storm and participate in its power.[9]

The Ju/wasi (San Bushmen) did not seek to influence the storm or call the rain as we agricultural and industrial peoples do. They sought resonance and power, just as I was taught to do in the Andes by "pulling down the lightning."

Small actions affect vast, complex systems in our living universe, where all is interconnected. We know this as the "butterfly effect," chaos theory's term for what happens when the "small" event—a butterfly flapping its wings in one part of the world—affects, over time, the weather systems in another part of the world, creating a tornado or hurricane.[10]

Similarly, your internal energetic states of alignment and resonance have effects beyond those around you: they reverberate throughout the world. Lauren C. Gorgo describes the law of resonance in action as "a process by which a higher vibrating body of energy will automatically cause a lower vibrating body of energy to match or align with its frequency ... think: tuning fork."[11] Think also of the "Hundredth Monkey" effect, morphic fields, and nonlocal changes in consciousness and learning: all these support the power of our choices and behavior.[12]

DOLPHIN DREAMS: LEARNING ALIGNMENT FROM OUR RELATIVES

In my snorkel and fins, I am moving slowly in deep, clear water. Below me, across the sandy bottom, the pod of spinner dolphins moves in unison, curving with sleek elegance around the bay. A young one swims between two adults. Three adults move smoothly across and around each other's bodies, touching and massaging while swimming. Another group of five moves toward the surface, back fins curving above the water as the group leaps, breathes, and dives down in unison.

I am, meanwhile, twisting and turning every which way to watch in wonder. As the dolphins swim toward me, I take a breath and dive to join them, curving and rotating my own body in mimicry, swimming underwater as fast as I can to keep up.

I know they notice me when they rise out of the water just in time for me to gasp for breath, but before their own lungs need air. I know they are playing with me when they swim up parallel to my body, a foot away, and look me in the eye as they slow to move at my speed. I know I have entered into their amazing energy field when their vast presence accompanies me for days, in and out of water.

Dolphins have a sensory, energetic intelligence far more highly developed than ours. They move in unison: rising, diving, turning as one. They are models of connectedness, of brain-body-awareness, of the fluidity of multiple organisms moving, thinking, and responding as a unit. Dolphins *live* in resonance and alignment.

Spinner dolphin pods midwife difficult humpback whale births, energetically massaging the mother whale by swimming spirals around her, never touching, to vibrate the water and ease her labor. Dolphins are known to identify rare genetic diseases and chromosomal abnormalities in human fetuses simply by swimming around the human mother.[13]

You can learn about spontaneous, instinctual, undomesticated, and resonant behavior by observing such wild creatures. They offer you lessons about play, fluidity, and vibrant aliveness.

Many believe that the dolphins and their humpback whale companions in the warm waters of Hawaii choose to contact humans, choose to come near them, choose to interact. Many also believe that dolphin/whale health and vitality are symbolic of and crucial to the survival and evolution of the planet. Muriel Lindsay, who has been exploring dolphin-human relationship for fifteen years, reports this message from the dolphins:

Our intent with you for millennia has been to inspire you so that you may know more of your creative potency. When we refer to your creativity, we also include the need for balance and not going overboard in any direction without correcting things in short order. We can tell by looking at your fields of energy, which we can easily see, how things are going with you. The degree to which we trust our feeling nature is what allows us to do this since that is our top priority, and has been the most prominent aspect on our evolutionary path.[14]

In other words, these wild creatures know things that we humans do not. What if we were able to hone our vibratory, energetic, resonant communications with each other to the level that is the dolphin norm?

Having learned the beauty of alignment, you are now ready to move on to reciprocity, the third pillar of perceptual change. In chapter 14 you will discover how the ancient, sacred practice of reciprocity informs every level of indigenous peoples' lives. You will think about reciprocity in a money economy and reciprocity in nature. You will learn practices you can explore to develop your own reciprocity and experience its transformative power.

CHAPTER 14
RECIPROCITY

Living in reciprocity changes your way of being in the world. It changes how you relate to everyone and everything. You move from dualistic thinking to interconnected experience. As Thich Nat Hanh says,

> *You carry Mother Earth within you. She is not outside of you. Mother Earth is not just your environment. In that insight of inter-being, it is possible to have real communication with the Earth, which is the highest form of prayer. In that kind of relationship you have enough love, strength, and awakening to change your life.*[1]

Reciprocity, or *ayni* in Quechua, is not just a principle but a feeling born from your heart. It flows from the cosmos and from love, the river of being.

You have been working with reciprocity all along in your travels through this book: every energy exchange—with a mountain or tree, air or water—involves reciprocity. The focus of this chapter is to help you build the third pillar of your perception. As you deepen your understanding and use of reciprocity, you will change your perceptions of relationships, responsibilities, and "reality" itself.

Exploring your reciprocal relationships with other creatures helps you go beyond your own skin; beyond your ego; beyond your self-centeredness; and beyond separation and isolation. When you live in and engage with an alive, pulsing universe, you find beauty and connection everywhere.

SACRED ENERGY EXCHANGE

You are always exchanging energy. When you breathe, you are exchanging energy with air (along with exchanging molecules of carbon dioxide for oxygen). When you greet someone, you are exchanging energy, along with your words and handshake or hug. Everything is energy, and the exchange happens whether or not you are conscious of it.

By perceiving energetic exchange as reciprocal and balanced—not giving too much or taking too much—you can significantly shift your experience of the world.

Energetic reciprocity is a sacred and mutual exchange of energy, appreciation, and respect. It is focused on maintaining balance and harmony between all living beings. Reciprocal exchange honors the interconnection of all beings: what you do affects the whole. "To practice *ayni* [reciprocity] with all people and all of nature is to open the heart."[2]

When reciprocity truly comes from your heart, there's no attachment to outcome. Instead there is focus on the flow of energy, mutuality, complementarity, the communal, and interrelationship.

As Q'ero Humberto Sonqo Quispé describes it, reciprocity "is a moving river of energy: releasing, drawing in, moving and dancing with the universe." To practice it, he advises us to "play, dance, open, receive, and give." [3]

The context, when everyone and everything is interconnected, is that what you give will be returned in some way. Maybe not by the same person. Maybe not at the same moment. Maybe even in a mysterious way. Think of the old saying for this: "What goes around, comes around."

As you have discovered, giving in a tightfisted or less than heartfull way comes back to you too! This is because all exchanges involve energy given and received. The quality of energy you offer—in speech, behavior, and reciprocal payment—is what returns to you. What you receive depends on your openness, fluidity, perception, and intent.

If your child gives you a leaf he picked up on his walk, his joy is in the sharing; he does not expect anything back. When my friends offer free healing clinics, their joy is in being of service and contributing to balance and harmony by making others' lives easier.

The perception that *an exchange*—whether offering, trade, assistance, appreciation, or purchase—*is a way of maintaining balance and harmony* is really different from our dominant attitude ("Me first!" "I want more!").

For example, one of the most powerful bonds within the social fabric of the Ju/wasi Bushmen was a partnership called *xaro*. Almost every person had a set of partners, some living far away, with whom he or she exchanged gifts over time. The gifts were small, handmade or traded. One person gave a gift; time passed. The recipient at some time—not right away, maybe six months or a year later—gave a gift in return. The gift giving cemented goodwill and fed the important cultural emphasis on sharing so that all had access to whatever food and resources were available.[4]

Reciprocity is more inclusive than the Western idea of "in-kind" responses to others. Western expectations of an equal favor, benefit, penalty, or emotional response in exchange for what is given are encoded in the Bible: "an eye for an eye, a tooth for a tooth." Meaning, if I give you something, you give me something back of equal or greater value. Yet when we look at the state of the planet, this biblical philosophy isn't working out so well. People feel alone, unsupported, and disconnected. Honor killings beget more honor killings, greed and violence escalate, and warfare is constant.

Acts of Reciprocity

Acts of reciprocity are acts of *connection*. When my friend brings me eggs and strawberries from her garden, she's gifting me with the work of her hands, the food of her soil, the relationship she has with her garden. Without words, all of this connects me to her and to her life in deep ways.

Acts of reciprocity are ways of acknowledging the *interconnection* of all things, all beings. You keep fresh water and seed for the birds because your life is enriched by their presence. You cultivate native plants because you know our planet depends on them; you know our insect and bird life will diversify in a symbiotic relationship. You leave offerings and make ceremony in pure gratitude for life. These simple actions can have profound meaning as you weave nature and cosmic connections into your life.

Acts of reciprocity *deepen our relationships.* When you take time to be reciprocal, especially with your nonhuman companions, you weave a thread that winds and expands in mysterious ways. Each time you leave a gift at a sacred place, you remember that place in detail. This means you can return there in imagination or journey, connect your filaments with that place, and know that place in your heart. It becomes part of your sacred circle; your world widens.

A spontaneous act of reciprocity is fun and makes you feel good. A red carnation handed to me in Oslo left me smiling for the entire day. In turn, of course, my smiling energy affected everyone I met.

Regular, daily, continuous reciprocity may not be so easy: why would you bother when everyone else is out for himself? It wasn't until I spent time with indigenous, non-Western people that I began to understand the transformative power of reciprocity, the reasons why we might bother, no matter what.

Developing a Reciprocal Perspective: Learning from Others

To help clarify the experience of reciprocity, one that may be foreign to you, I offer you a few examples from wisdom keepers around the world. The indigenous people in these examples model behavior and consciousness that embody reciprocity: giving before receiving, joyful connection with the living energies surrounding them, communal balance, and respect for both the seen and unseen.

The Holy Stone, Siberia

In *The Raven's Gift*, kayaker, scientist, and adventurer Jon Turk describes being rescued, healed, and befriended by Siberian people along the Kamchatka coast. He describes their classic way of perceiving and exchanging living energies in a reciprocal way:

> *Simon, the mayor, had told me that energy flows from the magma-filled bowls of the earth to the Holy Stone. At the same time, people absorb positive energy from the tundra and also feed it to the stone. Thus the stone is a focal point, a storage unit, and a transfer station for good energy. People give energy to the stone, but they also take energy. If I concentrate a little power from the landscape, modulate it through my body, and deliver it to the stone, then a friend, a stranger, or even an enemy can assimilate some of that goodwill, amplified by the receipt of additional energy from the deep earth. Simon had further explained that to receive energy from the earth, a person must be in tactile contact with it, by walking, skiing, living in a yuranga, or herding reindeer ... Without reciprocity, the Holy Stone will eventually lose its power.[5]*

Every indigenous culture has places like the Holy Stone—sacred places of ceremony and worship—where this exchange, giving and receiving, is practiced. Cultures formerly seen as "primitive" generally incorporate reciprocity throughout their daily lives. Western places of worship carry some of this focus—we pray, we get God's help—yet it is not perceived as reciprocity.

The Women of Mollomarca, Peru

Reciprocity is a seminal, operative principle of behavior and being in the Andes. Says Juan Nuñez del Prado, an initiated teacher of the Q'ero tradition,

> *... the more you give away your power, the more huaca, or sacred, you become ... The surest way to gain is when you are able to exchange energy with another living system. This is what keeps you and Pachamama (Mother Earth) alive.[6]*

He goes on to explain perceptions that mirror those in Siberia a half-world away:

> *Look at it on a simple level. When you appreciate someone, you are giving them some of your living energy. Receiving your energy, they will have more and be better able to give you some back later. This is a natural self-sustaining process of interdependence ... We keep nothing. We are here in the kay pacha (this world) to learn to do ayni (reciprocity).*[7]

Our assumptions, beliefs, and perceptions can run into a wall when they meet the different reciprocal ways of another culture head on. I experienced this personally a few years ago. In the Western world, we expect our donations to go to a specific program or have identifiable results: feeding the hungry, buying seed and farming tools for the dispossessed, building the new music center. In the Andes, I discovered that such contributions may follow a less linear and less outcome-oriented path.

People who traveled with our teacher Américo Yábar frequently visited the village of Mollomarca in the Eastern Andes. In this largely traditional Quechua farming village on the slopes of the mountains, there were few signs of Western encroachment: most spoke only Quechua and wore traditional handspun and woven garments. Only the mayor and a few other men spoke Spanish and wore Western pants and shirts.[8]

We were godparents to many babies, and had learned much from the people there; we wanted to practice reciprocity. Back home, we raised a considerable sum of money so the women could build their own building in the village. They had no communal, roofed space where they could weave together; huts were small and family focused.

Months later, we were surprised to hear that the women had shared half of our money with the men in the village. Because the men already had a gathering space, we reacted as if it represented yet another women-give-their-power-away situation. Yet from an anthropological and cultural perspective, reciprocity is so rooted in all aspects of these people's lives that *nothing* would be done to threaten the long-held and complex balance between men and women. Instead of short-term gain (the new weaving house), the women shared the money, avoiding resentment and maintaining long-term balance. They built a partial house with the remaining funds.

Among the Quechua and Aymara people, in *ayllu* (traditional communities) in Peru, Ecuador, and Bolivia, reciprocity is a traditional form of mutual help still practiced and institutionalized. It is deeply ingrained in their cultural identity and worldview on many levels. For example, half the *ayllu* is responsible one year for organizing community festivals, while the other half fulfills established support functions. The next year, the two halves trade roles. "Leadership," along with the cost and the honor of extra work, is shared, rotated, and kept in balance.

As Julia Meyerson says, "The indigenous Andean way of life is based on the idea that life regenerates itself through mutual nurturance and aid."[9] It is a bit like the American pioneer spirit: knowing that they could not survive without each other, neighbors gathered for barn raisings and sometimes for harvests. The difference is that American pioneers perceived themselves as separate from nature, both culturally and spiritually; in the indigenous world, the living energy and relatedness of all beings are foundational.

Reciprocity in Our Money Economy

Living in our money-based economy, it's a challenge to figure out how to practice reciprocity. It is a complex and charged topic, so I offer these examples as food for reflection on how you might incorporate reciprocity into your life.

When I was first learning *Vipassana* meditation, I attended a ten-day silent retreat with a world-famous teacher, S. N. Goenka, at a tent camp in the woods of Mendocino, California. We gathered in a huge rented tent for our five "sittings" a day, and were served two vegetarian meals daily by a volunteer kitchen crew. Teachers were not paid; experienced students offered service in gratitude for what the teachings had brought to them.

There was no charge, no fee for anything. We participants were simply asked to donate what we could at the end of the ten days. This was a surprising, welcome, and transformative experience for me. The *sanga* (community) actualized trust and reciprocity so that anyone could participate, and the whole community benefited.

Many indigenous spiritual leaders and healers—I think of Aama Bombo (Nepal), Mandaza Kandemwa (Zimbabwe), and Humberto Sonqo Quispé (Peru)—use their "earnings" in the West to benefit their communities and support large and extended compounds.[10] For example, they may feed the community (as happens in Zimbabwe, which for years has suffered severe economic stress), or build radio communications and schools (as is done in Peru). Little or no personal wealth is accumulated, and there is much personal sacrifice: doing healings and ceremony daily for weeks or months, and traveling extensively staying wherever space is made available and eating whatever is offered. In reciprocity and gratitude, the Westerners who sponsor, support, and organize these visits volunteer their time and resources.

Not every indigenous healer works this way, of course. And in our Western world—where marketing gurus and web-based coaches focus your attention on the ease of "making a six-figure income"—it is doubly difficult to honor principles of reciprocity. You are likely to think, "Maybe I'm being a sap, or stupid, for not charging more."

You must, of course, make your own decisions about how to incorporate reciprocity. There is no right way, and there is no judgment. There is the opportunity to shift your consciousness about the threads of giving and receiving and how you perceive them.

DEVELOPING A RECIPROCAL PERSPECTIVE: LEARNING FROM NATURE

All natural communities, or ecosystems, exist, thrive, and are based on reciprocal relationship. As you observe nature and explore connecting your heart and energetic filaments, you find pathways for living in awareness with the plants and creatures that inhabit the same space as you.

The more you extend your consciousness to different living beings in reciprocity, the more you feel supported, connected, and entwined with the world. Knowing "I am another yourself" with a tree, a stream, a mountain, or a salmon lets you "see" with different eyes, feel with different awareness, and experience a sublime unity consciousness where there is no separation between inside and outside. San Bushman hunter Nqate Xqamxebe explains,

> *When you track an animal, you must become the animal. Tracking is like dancing, because your body is happy—you can feel it in the dance and then you know that the hunting will be good. When you are doing these things you are talking with God.*[11]

FOREST

Reciprocity in a forest comes from evolutionary interrelationships developed over millennia: Tall trees shade and protect smaller plants, provide a wind buffer, and feed soil with composting, nutrient-rich leaves and branches. Roots hold soil intact from erosion, enable moisture retention, send water to nearby trees that have not received enough water, and recharge groundwater. Dense fern and groundcover keep soil damp, rich, and loose. Downed wood provides hiding places and homes for many creatures and food for others, from insects to mushrooms. Some species of trees, like tall redwoods, contain whole ecosystems in their high branches: specialized mice, ferns, birds, and insects who never touch ground. Observing these interrelationships can stimulate our experiential understanding of reciprocity.

BIRDS, BATS, AND BUGS

Away from cities and the artificial, nonnative planted worlds of suburbs and shopping centers, interconnections are more obvious. In the oak woodlands where I live, I watch each spring when the temperature warms enough for vast swarms of tiny insects to emerge. Their presence draws the tree swallows, who swoop and dive, feasting on them. Five kinds of woodpeckers harvest ants and bugs under the oak bark, but do not compete for food: each species' beak is designed slightly differently—longer, more curved, stronger, shorter—to access different bugs. Bats, similarly, arrive when mosquitos and other insect foods hatch.

Charles Darwin's observation of finches in the Galapagos Islands, cut off from mainland South America, began our scientific recording and understanding of such evolutionary processes. Yet, of course, humans have always observed, understood, and engaged with these processes for their survival.

LIVING IN A TREE

Thinking about Julia Butterfly Hill living high in an old growth redwood tree for more than a year, our minds may jump to fear—of cold, of the tree swaying in wild winter storms, of wet, of bugs, of whatever.[12] Our bodies can barely imagine what Julia experienced: the bliss of birdsong, the touch of shifting speckled sunlight on skin, the energizing electric stimulus of wind circulating negative ions all around. Or the deep familiar knowing that comes from lying next to tree bark each day, the energy flow between human and tree, the fullness of relationship. Once Julia's tree became family/familiar, her whole worldview shifted. The trees and the forest became not just abstractions to protect, but one of her relations. In her whole being, the forest became as important to honor and protect as a child or family member. The experience changed her life and her path.

WHALES SPEAK

Participating in my first Council of All Beings (see "Creating a Council of All Beings" (page 192)) more than thirty years ago gave me tools for deepening both connection and awareness. Later, shamanic journeying offered new pathways for learning. It is thus that I have had a long relationship with a whale teacher in what we call "nonordinary" reality. Asking this whale how the species could help us connect and weave their consciousness with ours, I was given this beautiful advice:

You know we circle the oceans in our migrations. We read the route using echolocation, with each other, the sea floor, and the ocean cur-

rents. We know the way, and we weave a web of connection throughout the ocean.

We need you to know how desperate our situation is. It is becoming much harder to survive. The krill (our food chain) are decimated; the less-cold upwelling is changing our environment; the net trawlers are competing with us; and the oil spills are polluting our waters. We need you to know that this is your situation, your oceans, your world as well as ours.

You can bring us light and love. You can be witness to our suffering and demise. You can make the connection and keep it, learning about our plight, seeing us as a part of you.

We are sacrificing ourselves so you can remember your world and put it back together. Every action helps. Every person's awareness helps. This is not a time to give up hope. Do not despair.

We feel our existence threatened by changes in global climate, just as you do. Our job is to maintain connection—with each other and with you—and we continue to do that. We offer you this opening into our dimension, our awareness. Please connect your hearts with ours. Please feel the light we weave as we swim and migrate. Please weave your own light. We are one.

When we perceive everything as having life force, we humans live in reciprocity: the deer, the vegetables, the trees, and the chickens—all our relations—give us food, warmth, tools; in turn, we honor them and treat them as relatives.

When everything has life force, keeping balance and harmony is essential: if one part of the world dies, everything is affected. When everything has life force, we humans see ourselves as part of the whole, interconnected, living in union. In our reciprocal exchange, we draw on and feed the "implicate, creative principle of the natural world."[13] Crowfoot, a Blackfoot warrior and orator expressed the whole in this way:

What is life? It is the flash of a firefly in the night. It is the breath of a buffalo in the wintertime. It is the little shadow which runs across the grass and loses itself in the sunset.[14]

Practicing Reciprocity

Reciprocity is an attitude and practice you can carry into all parts of your life. Seeing beauty, you can feel grateful or write a poem. Growing tomatoes, you can give them tender care. Loving wild creatures, you can act for their protection.

Throughout this book you have found exercises that engage your reciprocity—physical, energetic, and spiritual—deeply. More practices follow for enhancing your reciprocal perceptions.

LEAVING SIMPLE OFFERINGS

All around the world people make daily offerings to trees, mountains, ancestors, and spirit: incense on the altar (in Japan), fresh flowers at the "spirit house" (Indonesia), chalk designs by the front door (in India), stones added to *chortens* and *apachetas* at mountain passes (in the Himalayas and Andes). Leaving such an offering creates a visual, energetic connection—a thread.

Have you ever been curious about or inspired by seeing such offerings when you traveled, or on your home turf?

There's a fence post on a trail near my house where hikers leave found bird feathers. There's a cleft in a rock above the Golden Gate Bridge where passersby place pinecones, stones, and tiny flowers. When you see these acts of reciprocity, your heart sings. When you make these acts of reciprocity yourself, your world changes.

> Follow your intuition and be spontaneous! Leave a found object in a tree or on a rock where others will see it and be inspired. Make a small offering with flowers or feathers. Give something to your favorite tree each time you pass.

Global Meditations

Even if you are not a regular meditator, there are numerous opportunities to join with others around the globe to feed peace and be witness to the need for change. Knowing that so many others are focusing their energy and love at the same moment can be transformative. Such

energetic exchanges feed your soul as well as the intent we hold collectively.[15]

CREATING A COUNCIL OF ALL BEINGS

This group council was developed by Buddhist teacher and systems
theorist Joanna Macy, along with deep ecologist John Seed, and has
been taught all over the world.[16]

The Council of All Beings helps participants directly experience
the voices and wisdom of the creatures with whom we share this earth.
Any sized group, whether four or forty, can create such a council to
allow other life forms to speak through them.

Each person in the group chooses a creature, plant, tree, or some
other living being to connect with. The intent is to listen to and perceive from that creature's perspective. (This is similar to what is called
shapeshifting in shamanic work.)

In a deep meditative place, each person seeks a living being, asks
permission, and becomes that being, seeing through her eyes, running
and moving with her body, experiencing the world through her.

Each participant brings her being's wisdom back to the Council
and speaks from the perspective of that being. Instead of humans
talking, everyone listens to representatives of trees, animals, wilde-
beests, bumblebees, alpine flowers, and green sea turtles speaking
in council. The experience takes you into the larger world of which
we are all a part, what Buddhists call interbeing: the interconnectedness that you know and speak about but do not often experience.
Sitting in such a Council of All Beings is yet another way to step into
an energetic field.

Create your sacred circle, your group's sacred space.

Offer these instructions:

Everyone will listen in silence for the single nonhuman—animal,
plant, feature of the landscape—who wants to speak through her.
(Present this as a "role play," an "exercise in moral imagination,"
as shamanic, or as practicing what it would feel like to see the
world from another creature's perspective—whatever works for
your group.)

Explain that after the silent listening period, each person will introduce themselves as their ally—e.g., "I am snake and I live close to the Earth,"—and will let their ally express itself in any way it wants to, including movements and noises it likes to make.

Instruct everyone to refer to humans as "they" or "the two-leggeds." That is, don't talk to the other creatures in the circle as if they were human, for this is very confusing for them. Everyone will maintain the connection, sensibility, and feeling of their creature throughout the Council.

Process:

During a period of silence or soft drumming or rattling (for twenty to thirty minutes, or a shorter time with children), each individual listens carefully to the voice of their creature, asking what the being wants to share with the group.

At the end of the silent period, invite people to speak in the voice of their creature (not *for* the creature, but *as* the creature) using the "first person" voice. Only the creatures will speak, not the humans.

When the circle of sharing is completed, invite participants to thank their ally silently, release their connection, and return fully to themselves.

You will notice that the feeling in the group will deepen, and deepen again, as the creatures speak. Listening to Whale and Goldfinch, Yellow Violet and Blue Oak, Salamander and Dolphin literally drops you into their world. You shed your solely human identification and feel deep empathy for the myriad species and landscapes of the Earth. The messages and perceptions of these creatures fill your heart and empower your reciprocity and compassion.

The more sacred and focused the Council space is, the deeper you go. Yet this does not have to be overtly spiritual. All that is required of a group is the intent to experience another living being as fully as possible.

Reciprocity in Ceremony

Participating in earth-honoring ceremony is a wonderful way to express an attitude of reciprocity. It is also a way to experience and see energy moving. Even if at first you simply go through the motions and learn the ropes—the patterns of a fire ceremony or the process of creating a group offering, for example—your *experience* helps you engage your heart and body. The more you can feel with your senses how the energy changes, just as you do when visiting a place again and again, the more you can perceive the power of ceremony.

This ancient reality is confirmed by placebo neuroscientists. Fabrizio Benedetti at the University of Turin writes,

> ... *therapeutic rituals move a lot of molecules in the patient's brain, and these molecules are the very same as those activated by the drugs we give in routine clinical practice. In other words, rituals and drugs use the very same biochemical pathways to influence the patient's brain.*[17]

As Mayan Ajq'ij OmeAkaEhekatl Erick Gonzales explains,

> *Traditionally, indigenous people have kept the clans strong and united by continuously having ceremonial gatherings to keep the people together with one mind and one heart, supporting the crystallization of their visions ... our councils put us together with the spiritual, the elemental, and the natural world, and that is why our people always gather in sacred councils. Not only to share with each other, but to be present to share with the spiritual and natural beings of life.*[18]

Juan Nuñez del Prado tells us that ceremonies "are a way to stimulate our seeds. They are a way to learn from both teachers and the collective unconscious." [19]

One way to learn how to engage in ceremonial reciprocity is to participate in traditional ceremonies. The elders carry the power of tradition and community, as well as their own deep learning, helping you engage with the particular tradition. Leaders guide the focus, offerings, prayers, dancing and drumming, and intent. Participants add their prayers and intent. Depending on the particular tradition and leaders, participants may be expected to remain observers, be fully engaged, or something in between.

Another way to learn is by creating your own ceremonies. You can set your focus and intent and create rituals drawing on traditions you have learned and your own experience. The power that comes from everyone's engagement and participation is transformative, and deepens over time. As with all experiential processes, the more you do it, the stronger and more confident you become, and the more excited the spirits are to help you along.

THE TRANSFORMATIVE POWER OF RECIPROCITY

When you know you are related to the animals and plants who feed you, the ancestors who watch over you, the mountains that gather rainclouds to water your crops, and the spirits who teach you, you are inspired, even compelled, to acknowledge and honor them, to express your appreciation and gratitude.

Astronaut Edgar Mitchell, upon seeing Earth from space, had his heart opened:

> As he approached the planet we know as home, he was filled with an inner conviction as certain as any mathematical equation he'd ever solved. He knew that the beautiful blue world to which he was returning is part of a living system, harmonious and whole—and that we all participate, as he expressed it later, "in a universe of consciousness." He became convinced that the uncharted territory of the human mind was the next frontier to explore, and that it contained possibilities we had hardly begun to imagine. Within two years of his expedition, Edgar Mitchell founded the Institute of Noetic Sciences in 1973.[20]

Similarly, divers who have freed a whale from fishing nets describe the transformative moment when they and the whale looked into one another's eyes.

Living in reciprocity helps bring everything into balance and harmony. It is a way of stepping into the future and creating a world your descendants will welcome: a world of abundance and connection. It's a way of shifting your vibration and moving yourself into what some have called *homo luminous*, the possible successor to *homo sapiens*.

To come into right relationship with the earth is to see and experience yourself in resonance with all beings, geologic and magnetic energies, and the whole cosmos. In this state, you learn more and more how to live in resonance and care for your earth, your Pachamama. As poet Wendell Berry writes,

> ... *Ask the questions that have no answers.*
> *Invest in the millennium. Plant sequoias.*
> *Say that your main crop is the forest*
> *that you did not plant,*
> *that you will not live to harvest.*
>
> *Say that the leaves are harvested*
> *when they have rotted into the mold.*
> *Call that profit. Prophesy such returns.*
> *Put your faith in the two inches of humus*
> *that will build under the trees*
> *every thousand years ...*[21]

Shamanic Connection with Mystical Worlds

At the heart of all shamanic traditions, worldwide, is reciprocal connection. The forces of the natural world, the elements, and the spirits of plants and animals are engaged in sacred, loving relationship to solve problems, perform healing, help you learn about the other dimensions, and return the world to balance. In this way, shamanic healing is energy healing.

For more than fifty thousand years, humans have maintained such relationships in the "nonordinary worlds" that are parallel to the ordinary world you live and breathe in. These worlds are also known through myth, dream, and vision. You can deepen all of the practices, principles, and experiences in this book through the shamanic practice of seeing from the heart.

Aspects of this practice include ceremony, shamanic journeying, learning through direct revelation, and developing reciprocal relationships with both earth and spirit. They help you develop your power and find your way back into harmony with the universe and your own soul. They help you nurture the planet. They help you find your true essence as a being in this interconnected world.

The learning of shamanism and shamanic journeying is the focus of many workshops, ceremonies, cultural immersions, and books.[22] The ceremony I want to share, which comes from the traditional healer Mandaza Kandemwa, exemplifies the substance of indigenous people's relationships with the living beings of earth, spirit, and cosmos.

Mandaza carries both the Svikiro traditional healer and Mhondoro peacemaker traditions from Zimbabwe. A few years ago I asked for his help in making offerings to the star beings, and developing a relationship with them. Mandaza said to me "Earth, Water, and the Star People are the three legs of your stool" (the stool is an important practical and metaphorical symbol in most of Africa). He suggested this ceremony—prayers and offerings for me to make—for each of the three "legs."

As you will see, the connections made in this ceremony are comprehensive; they focus on surrender, obstacles, mistakes, forgiveness, assistance, and reciprocity. They are also profoundly healing, deepening, and mysterious. You can use the form of this ceremony to deepen your own connections and relationships.

CEREMONY OF RECIPROCITY WITH EARTH, WATER, AND STAR PEOPLE

Go to a mountain and surrender to spirits. In surrendering, you are saying to them, "I know nothing about your ways. I want to make body and heart an empty vehicle, an unpolluted temple, for spirit."

Let go of obstacles in heart, mind, and spirit.

Ask for forgiveness for whatever wrong you did as a human.

Ask the good spirits above to heal you physically and spiritually.

Ask the spirits to give you clear sleeping dreams, visions, and messages that do not need interpretation.

Ask them to be your teachers.

As you pray, throw the offerings in six directions: North, South, East, West, Above, and Below.

For the Star People Spirits, make offerings from a mountaintop.

For the Water Spirits, make offerings to a river, ocean, or lake.

For the Earth Spirits, make offerings to the six directions while sitting under a tree.

Once you have made your offerings, jump into the water for initiation by the spirits, immersing yourself multiple times.[23]

In this chapter you have explored reciprocity, discovering how it transforms the way you relate to everyone and everything and strengthens the pillars of your perception. In the next chapter, I invite you to open to your receptivity like a flower. You will reflect on the barriers that keep you from receiving as much as you are given; explore the ways in which listening, witnessing, language, trust, and dreaming open portals of possibility for you; and build the fourth pillar of your perception.

CHAPTER 15
RECEPTIVITY

Receptivity expresses your willingness to experience, engage, and be open. It is like a permeable membrane in your energy field, allowing what is unfamiliar or new into your awareness. Being receptive helps you look for commonalities—what you might share with others—and complementarities. Being receptive helps you step aside from judgment and your experience of separation.

Receptivity opens you to possibilities not yet explored, and different ways of perceiving your experience. Maybe compliments usually pass you by—you hear the words but just don't feel them or take them in. Possibly you are so busy you forget to slow down and enjoy a hug someone gives you. Most of us are not so good at receiving: our stories and interpretations of reality cloud or misinterpret what is actually going on. Won't it be wonderful to build this pillar of your perception so you can fully take in and receive all the blessings that come your way?

As you've explored practices for changing your energy, you have been becoming more receptive. The focus of this chapter is to help you change your perceptions of relationships, responsibilities, and "reality" itself as you deepen your use and understanding of receptivity.

Without receptivity, we do not trust enough to listen and hear. Without receptivity, we spiral within what we already know: our minds cycle their old stories and tell us what we think; we repeat our beliefs endlessly in our conversations; and we refuse to believe what does not correspond with our ideas. Our perception of the world remains static and rigid. Nothing can move.

Lack of receptivity creates a barrier, a kind of wall around us. We unconsciously hope this wall will keep things as they are, prevent disruption, and protect us from having to change.

We know that such rigidity of beliefs has personal physical, psychological, spiritual, and health consequences. It can result in disease, fear, suffering, despair, and uncontrollable rage. We also know that rigid belief systems are the source of increasing national, cultural, and species dysfunction—whether in the form of climate change denial or cultural-religious wars over what is the right way to live.

Nothing will change until we perceive a different road, and take it. The first step is to be receptive to different possibilities. Then our willingness to try something new, hear something different, and experience a shift will open the pathways that lead to those possibilities.

For our personal health and our species' survival, it makes sense to cultivate receptivity.

OUR BARRIERS OF RESISTANCE

"Don't believe everything you think," says a bumper sticker someone once gave me for my car. I like to think of myself as a receptive person. Yet I can attest to many times when my own unconscious barriers impeded shifts I was trying to make.

Some years ago I began a practice of transfiguration.[1] Each morning before rising I'd find the light in my heart, a small golden light, and see it getting bigger and bigger until it filled my whole aura, my energy bubble. I was learning to find, experience, and become my true essence. Perceiving from that place changed everything.

Yet I wondered why I had to start over each day: Why wasn't it easier as the feelings became more familiar? What was keeping me from maintaining a transfigured state, as well-known spiritual leaders and saints do? Of course, I wasn't trying to be a saint; rather, I wanted to live from my true essence, and not just from the persona I had developed.

This is the same issue that anyone who is changing their perceptual framework or cultivating a spiritual practice faces. Even when you have a supportive community, feel transported in body and spirit, and experience how your practice eases your life, you struggle and resist.

Spiritual teacher Sandra Ingerman often says, "You have to be able to receive love in order to give love."[2] While I had heard this often, one day I *understood* that I had been focusing outward rather than experiencing the reciprocal flow of energy. I was not consciously receiving, or even perceiving, what was being sent my way.

I began to explore—consciously—how to receive and how to be receptive. What I discovered was barriers—in my thinking, habits, trust, and unconscious assumptions—that got in the way of my being receptive.

One barrier is belief. When you do not believe you are lovable or worthy of love, for whatever reasons, it is pretty hard to receive love.

A second barrier is lack of trust. When you assume that you are separate from others, that you are in competition, or that others are more capable than you are, you are not likely to trust that they are supporting you; you are not likely to receive their love or compliments.

A third barrier is habits of response. When someone says, "That's a pretty dress," and you reply, "Oh, it's old," you are discounting the compliment you just received. When the boss says, "Great job," and you doubt his intentions, your habits of response—the shadows of old patterns—are getting in the way of your being receptive. They are keeping you from enjoying the moment.

A fourth barrier lies in disconnection. When you don't experience the aliveness and consciousness in a plant, redwood, or hummingbird, it doesn't occur to you that they might be giving back to you.

We have myriad ways of being unreceptive. Excuses, confusion, ego, illusions, disbelief, and blame are habits to watch for. The "thick armor of doubt and skepticism that exists in the conscious mind" must be bypassed.[3] The unconscious beliefs, which are even stronger, have to be identified. As Dr. Bernie S. Siegel says, "people are addicted to their beliefs" even when they *know* a change would be better for them or the world.[4]

BELIEF AND DISBELIEF

Your perceptions come from far more than your thinking, conscious mind. Your preverbal brain—the limbic brain, the one without words—contains your childhood experiences, subconscious learning-by-example from your family, and the residue of any traumatic experiences (violence, rape, abandonment, addiction, and so on) you may have endured. Your heart and your body remember what your mind may not. Any of these preverbal, somatic memories can sabotage what you think you want to happen; affirmations cannot work when the subconscious mind and old beliefs hold sway.

As Gregg Braden writes,

> *Just the way sound creates visible waves as it travels through a droplet of water, our "belief waves" ripple through the quantum fabric of the universe to become our bodies and the healing, abundance, and peace—or disease, lack, and suffering—that we experience in life. And just the way we can tune a sound to change its patterns, we can tune our beliefs to preserve or destroy all that we cherish, including life itself.*[5]

When you address your preverbal sabotaging beliefs, you can step toward the creativity, radiance, and change that are your essence. This is where your intent, your choices, and your receptivity help you engage.

A good example is when you work with a personal coach, minister, or counselor: they can guide you for months, but if you don't try the new approach, the new behavior toward which they are guiding you, not much changes. If you are not receptive to suggestion and possibility, if you refuse the physician's medicine or the counselor's prescriptions, you are saying, "I really do not want to change my belief." Your old habits and behaviors become more embedded.

Essentially, you have to experience a difference in order to believe in it.

In *The Holographic Universe*, Michael Talbot writes extensively about the placebo effect. Miracles of healing occur when you put aside your normal assumptions about power, proof, knowledge, and your place in universe. In essence, Talbot says, "... our ability to control the body holographic is molded by our beliefs.[6]

CONFUSION

Confusion "protects" you from taking action. It can be exhausting and addictive: if you tell yourself you are confused and don't know what to do, you can wallow and avoid doing anything.

Confusion is often a mask, hiding your primary feelings, your *mad, sad, glad,* or *afraid* responses.

As Mark Wolynn of The Hellinger Institute writes,

When grief is overwhelming, we are rarely able to complete its process. Instead, we remain frozen in secondary emotions, unable to access the very emotions that will bring us relief. We develop unconscious strategies—anger, numbness, addictions to substances, exercise or work—designed to keep us going, but often these strategies serve only to keep us stuck. Unfortunately, our children learn too well from us and often repeat our patterns. We see time and time again how an individual's unresolved grief becomes the family's unresolved grief, and continues from generation to generation ... Yet, when we look back at the tragic events that devastated our families and remember those who suffered, and acknowledge them with great respect, we can begin to experience immediate relief. If we were to imagine the posthumous wishes of our dead ancestors, they would want only happiness and peace for us.[7]

We see confusion and inaction masking despair and powerlessness on a global scale in people's responses to community violence, global warming, and the effects of nuclear radioactivity. We see confusion and inaction masking despair and powerlessness on a personal level in our response to alcoholic siblings, friends who demean and bully others, or our own inability to speak our truth.

It is a huge shift of consciousness to step out of confusion by identifying and experiencing your feelings directly. It releases energy and frees you from a kind of internal entrapment when you ask yourself, "Am I mad, sad, glad, or afraid?" When you identify your primary feeling, you can rest in it, or decide what you want to do about it, rather than exhausting yourself with confusion. Stepping into the energy of your primary feelings gives you great power and internal authority. As Carolyn Myss expresses this,

From an energy point of view, every choice that enhances our spirits strengthens our energy field; and the stronger our energy field, the fewer our connections to negative people and experiences.[8]

DUALISTIC THINKING

Dualistic thinking—where you see only two possibilities, no middle ground, and no continuum of possibility—keeps you stuck. It reinforces cultural, religious, and political "truths" that are really just belief systems. As Jelalludin Rumi said nearly a thousand years ago,

> *If you think there are important differences or divisions between Jews, Christians, Hindus, Buddhists, and Muslims, then you are dividing yourself, between your heart—what you love with—and how you act in the world.*[9]

Many of us experience duality in thinking about our relationships and work: "If I leave this marriage, my life will be over." "I hate this job, but I'll never find another one in this economic climate." "No, I can't travel/go to school/learn a new skill because I have to take care of my child." None of these statements, which we so often hear, allows for any range of possibility or energetic change.

You see dualistic thinking even in young children. In first grade, for example, many children who are perfectly competent "artists"—in drawing, creating, painting, building—stop. Entirely. Why? Because the teacher praised someone else, or another child in the class does it "better." Seven-year-olds do tend toward black-and-white thinking because their brains are not yet fully developed. Yet when a mother reprimands her young daughter for some naughty behavior, and the child keeps repeating, "I'm a good girl. I'm a good girl," she cannot allow the possibility of "bad," let alone a mistake in behavior. How many of us secretly carry those kinds of thoughts into adulthood?

To shift into a more receptive frame of mind, you might consider a one-step-at-a-time approach. You might agree to try a different experience. You might explore complementarity, trying to discover how the "opposites" actually depend on and complement each other. The complementarity of the sexes, the reality that we cannot fully experience joy unless we have had some sorrow, and the well-known principle that the shadows in our emotional experience teach us how to be whole: all these examples of complementarity can work to modulate our dualistic thinking.

PORTALS OF POSSIBILITY FOR YOU

You can enhance your receptivity by developing the qualities of listening and witnessing. You can shift your receptivity in the ways you use language and trust your insights. Arundhati Roy's words convey the sensory, felt aspect of listening and feeling our way into receptivity: "Another world is not only possible, she is on her way. On a quiet day, I can hear her breathing."[10]

LISTENING

Listening from your three centers—belly, heart, and third eye—is central to developing receptivity. When you align your power, love, and vision in those three centers so your feelings and perceptions are not in conflict, receptivity flows. When you trust the experiences from all three centers (and avoid valuing only what is in your mind), you empower your whole being.

If, in contrast, your mind believes one thing and your heart feels another, you will experience conflict; it will be a challenge to be receptive. If your ego doubts, hope will be a challenge. If your heart is afraid, your body will close down and be unreceptive.

As Cynthia Sue Larson says,

Finding a state of deep listening ... of deep conversation ... without imposing old preexisting views or conforming to others' views is a transformative state of consciousness. From such a place, it is possible to more fully appreciate and become aware of all aspects of oneself, including our past and future selves. It is also possible to move past a sense that it is always the other person who is wrong or prejudiced and not listening ... so we can become alert and attentive to the way our minds sometimes move away from what we think may disturb us.[11]

In listening deeply, you suspend your self-oriented, reactive thinking, and instead listen with care and generosity; you trust that whatever others say, it comes from something true in their experience. You learn to do this by listening from your three centers.[12]

WITNESSING

Witnessing—observing what is, without judgment, reaction, or attachment—is another aspect of receptivity. You can learn the power of witnessing from many ancient spiritual traditions: every tradition of meditation, yoga, shamanism, and martial arts teaches the practice of witnessing.

Because judgment and reactivity cloud your mind, developing nonattachment is essential. Removing the distraction of wanting—things, people, qualities—helps you witness with your belly, heart, and vision fully open. As was advised in the *Yoga Sutras of Patanjali*, written between 400 BCE and 500 CE,

> *Practice leads you in the right direction, while non-attachment allows you to continue the inner journey without getting sidetracked into the pains and pleasures along the way.*[13]

And as the Dalai Lama expresses it, "Attachment is the origin, the root of suffering; hence it is the cause of suffering."[14]

In the Japanese martial art of *aikido*, you learn to witness and observe the energy of the opponent in order to use it. If someone is rushing toward you with anger or in fight mode, instead of trying to block or meet their energy head on, you step aside and redirect the opponent's energy, helping move them past you without injury.

Similarly, in shamanic practices around the world, witnessing what is, listening for what is needed to bring things into balance, and practicing nonattachment are central to all interactions with the unseen spirit worlds.[15]

"Neutrality" is the word Maori healers use for letting everything go, witnessing, and working without reaction or judgment.

Learning to witness without attachment to outcome shifts your receptivity and opens portals to different ways of organizing, identifying, and interpreting your experience. When you change your perception of the events you experience, you alter the way these situations live within you. When you no longer see yourself as the cause and effect of everything, you can also release the burden of having to fix it all. Instead, you can witness what is, see life flowing around and within you, and experience great relief.

Languaging

The way you use language can also shift your receptivity. The words you speak and tell yourself alter your perception.

For example, to say, "I am another yourself" (*In La'kesh*) feeds your awareness and vibration differently from saying "I am alone in the universe."

When you learn a friend has cancer, if you say, "I see you in your radiance during this challenge" rather than "Oh, that is so terrible," you are feeding hope rather than fear.

Every thought you have and every sentence you utter takes you closer to your vision or away from it. Becoming more and more conscious of your thoughts and language helps move you toward wider, heartfelt perception.

You can also fill the day with blessings to change the energy, feeling, intent, and perception with which you meet your life. As Pierre Pradervand suggests,

> *Spontaneous blessing is a flowing fountain that, like a mountain stream, cascades and sings. It expresses perpetual morning—defined as freshness, openness, gratitude, inspiration, newness, alertness, expectation of good, wakefulness, fresh beginning, purity, threshold, (re) birth, joy, innocence, and wonder.[16]*

Trusting and Dreaming

Sometimes the insights you are given as a result of your receptivity do not fit into any way of perceiving or understanding known to you. When this happens, having trust—that meaning will be revealed, that you are not crazy, that your inner experience is reliable, and that you do have inner authority to interpret the world—is crucial. As David Sparenberg expresses this,

> *That foundational necessity is this: We are each in need of relearning, and ever so deeply, to trust—trust the vulnerability of the heart, trust the creative guidance and visionary wisdom of the soul, trust spirit, trust Earth and, in the maelstrom of crisis and insecurity, to trust one another.[17]*

An experience I had many years ago illustrates this process of trusting insights and dreams without fully understanding their meaning. In a dream, I was walking along the Milky Way. There were others beside and near me, yet I did not know them. The starry path was beautiful. I understood that I was to keep walking along this path, and had no idea where I was going.

On waking, I knew this to be a potent, powerful dream of portent. I understood that I was to "walk the Milky Way path" in my everyday life, even as I had no clue what that meant.

Some years later, I happened to read that Mayan people refer to the Milky Way path as *Saq'Be*.' This was a clue: people before me had recognized this path. Gradually I found interviews in which ancient wisdom keepers from around the world spoke of their "star ancestors" and "coming from the stars." Realizing that other cultures perceive and hold a very different ancestral reality was another clue. Receptivity and trust carried me forward.

I continued to pay attention and be receptive to any bit of information I read or heard about star beings and the star path. My intent was to learn what I could: I wanted to know what my dream meant! I liked imagining and thinking about coming from the stars, but did not speak of this to anyone. I *assumed* and feared that my Milky Way path would be discounted and people would make fun of it.

After some years, I received spirit guidance to make offerings to the "star beings." I was told these offerings should be despachos (a traditional Andean ceremony). I was shown what to put in them and where to create them: on the mountains around the San Francisco Bay where I live, and in the Himalayas where I was about to travel. I was encouraged to invite others to participate in these ceremonies. All this clear guidance helped me continue to be receptive, listen, and witness the unfolding. I began to make the offerings on the mountains with small groups of people.

Learning the Milky Way path became for me a continual teaching about trusting, dreaming, and being receptive. I had to overcome my boulders of belief, my hesitancy and uncertainty. I had to keep putting aside habits of self-doubt and self-protection. I had to shift from thinking, *I don't know what I am doing* to allowing myself to experience the beauty of the offerings. Each offering I created, along with people's enthusiasm to join me, encouraged the next. When I understood enough to write about the thirteen or so star despachos I had made, I also encouraged people around the world to make their own. This process continues. And I know, now, that writing this book—guiding you into living in the heart of the universe as I have done—is part of the Milky Way path.

In trusting this path, I let my long training in and practice of reciprocity feed my intent. My perception—of our connections to the stars, of what is possible, of how the energy in the universe can feed our creativity—expanded as I continued to engage my receptivity and align with my vision.

You, too, will expand your receptivity as you move aside your barriers and open the doors to listening, witnessing, languaging, trusting, and dreaming. In turn, the flowering of your perceptions will naturally guide you into an experience of the earth and the universe as your extended body. I invite you now, in the final chapter, to circle around to where you started, reflecting on how you have learned to live in the heart of the universe.

Chapter 16
Weaving the Heart
of the Universe
into Your Life

Your visceral experience of the universe as alive, aware, and interconnected—with you, me, and everything surrounding us—is a great gift. No longer limited to thinking about such ideas, you now have the tools and practices to shift your perception, your energy, and your vision. You have learned many wonderful ways to expand your relationship with earth and the cosmos. Congratulate yourself: you are already dreaming a different world from the one you were dreaming when you first opened this book.

The power of being in connection, present with what is—whether it's ecstatic or scary, expanding or falling apart—brings balance to your heart. The power of focusing your attention and moving your energy makes you as fluid as a river, ready to meet any challenge.

As you continue to expand your perceptions—feeding the energy of beauty and hope, magic and possibility, and the mythic and spiritual aspects of your experience—each step moves you toward connecting your energy and changing your life. As you change yourself, you change your relationships and the world around you. You join your filaments with many others in weaving a grand pattern of cosmic harmony, resonance, and balance.

As you move on beyond this book—or return to it again—you will continue to connect with earth, cosmos, and all living beings. You will deepen your connections with the heart of the universe. And one day, you will realize that you live in the heart: it's your home.

Endnotes

Preface

[1] Our Milky Way is now known to be one of many galaxies in the supercluster Laniakea, which contains more than 100,000 galaxies and stretches 500 million light years across. By mapping thousands of galaxies, a team discovered Laniakea. Tully, R. Brent, Hélène Courtois, Yehuda Hoffman & Daniel Pomarède. "The Laniakea supercluster of galaxies." *Nature* 513, 04 September 2014. 71–73. 03 September 2014. http://www.nature.com/nature/journal/v513/n7516/full/nature13674.html. For images, see http://www.vox.com/2014/9/4/6105631/map-galaxy-supercluster-laniakea-milky-way.

Introduction

[1] Barrios, Carlos, *The Mayan Calendar: The World will Not End*. Santa Fe, NM, lecture. http://www.seri-worldwide.org/id435.html.

[2] I teach Energy Alchemy privately, in workshops, and online. See http://megbeeler.com.

[3] Wangyal, Tenzin. *Healing with Form, Energy, and Light: The Five Elements in Tibetan Shamanism, Tantra, and Dzogchen*. (Ithaca, New York: Snow Lion Press, 2002), xviii.

[4] Maya, Hopi, Q'ero, Cherokee, Tayta, Xingue, Seneca, Inuit, and Mapuche are among the indigenous peoples who prophesied the turning over of the world as we know it.

[5] In the 1940s, the Q'ero observed that a high-altitude mountain plant was disappearing; their Alpaca and Vicuña herds depended on this plant for forage. The water supply was diminishing; glaciers were shrinking. These events—what we now understand to be early evidence of climate change—triggered their prophesy of the turning over of the world as we know it (Pachacuti) and their responsibility to share long-protected teachings. When they intentionally came out of their isolated (fifteen- to seventeen-thousand foot) mountains in 1949, appearing at the annual Festival of the Virgin in Paucartambo, the closest town, the Q'ero were recognized by anthropologist Oscar Nunez del Prado (father of Juan Nunez del Prado) as bloodline descendants of the Inca. Since then, Q'ero wisdom keepers have reached out to people around the globe, sharing perception, cosmovision, and ceremony as a way of helping all humans make choices about our direction on the planet.

[6] "Akasha is a Sanskrit word meaning 'ether, space, or sky.' The root, kash, means 'to radiate or shine.' In Buddhism, the Akasha translates as 'infinite space,' a place that is without matter or any physical consistency. There is no time or space in the Akashic dimension; all timelines exist together simultaneously." The popular twenty-first-century understanding of the term Akashic records is "a place or dimension where we can create new realities, advance our skills, learn life lessons, and heal. A place of our own that we can quickly access through our own energy." Smith, Jacki and Patty Shaw. *Do It Yourself Akashic Wisdom: Access to the Library of Your Soul*. (San Francisco: Weiser Books, 2013), 3–5.

[7] In physicist David Bohm's view, the deeper and more fundamental order of reality of the universe—in contrast to the abstractions humans normally perceive—looks different when space and time are no longer the dominant factors determining relationships. Bohm coined the words "implicate" and "enfolded" to describe the deeper reality.

[8] Spirit guides like my Star Goddess are beings in the nonordinary worlds with whom we maintain a loving, reciprocal relationship. Also referred to as power animals and teachers, they may communicate during shamanic journeys, vision quests, and meditation. Personal communication, November 2010.

[9] Hahn, Thich Nhat. Beyond environment: falling back in love with Mother Earth. *The Guardian*. 20 February 2012. http://www.theguardian.com/sustainable-business/zen-thich-naht-hanh-buddhidm-business-values.

[10] Coined "nature deficit disorder" by Richard Louv, our separation has become culture wide and systemic. See Louv, Richard. *Last Child in the Woods: Saving our Children from Nature-Deficit Disorder*. Chapel Hill: Algonquin Books, 2005.

[11] Bahro, Rudolf. Quoted in Wheatley, Margaret, *The Place Beyond Fear and Hope*. *Lion's Roar*, March 2009. http://www.lionsroar.com/the-place-beyond-fear-and-hope/.

[12] Brother John. Society for the Study of Shamanism Conference, San Rafael, CA, September. 2014. Presentation.

[13] Hardy, Malcolm and Steve Heyes. *Beginning Psychology*. (5th ed). (Oxford University Press, 1999), 24–27.

[14] Dispenza, Dr. Joe. "How to evolve our brain to experiment a new reality? Stepping into the unknown." Interviewed by Lilou Mace (see www.LilouMace.com, previously www.JuicyLivingTour.com). YouTube. 8 June 2011. https://www.youtube.com/watch?v=0XcCoDlVf-s.

[15] Ingerman, Sandra, *Transmutation News*, February 2008. http://www.sandraingerman.com/transmutationnews.html.

[16] Chopra, Deepak, "Foreword", in Elgin, Duane. *The Living Universe: Where Are We? Who Are We? Where Are We Going?* (San Francisco: Berrett-Koehler Publishers, Inc., 2009), p.ix.

CHAPTER 1

[1] Américo Yábar learned the "eating hucha" process from Don Benito Qoriwayman, a famous teacher from Huasao near Cusco.

[2] In contrast with cosmovision, cosmology is the scientific study of the origin and structure of the universe, describing theories about the nature of the universe rather than direct experience of it.

[3] Despacho is the commonly used Spanish word for these offerings; in Quechua they are called *haywarisqa*. To learn more about creating a despacho, and the star despachos referred to in chapter 15, see Beeler, Meg, *The Shimmering World*, and *The Despacho Ceremony*. http://megbeeler.com.

[4] There is enigma at the heart of the stone gift. It came to me as physical object, yet it set in motion a pattern, a filament of connection that led down many pathways. The stone informed my healing, my vision, and my teaching; it fed me, and I fed it in return. It drew others to me who became apprentices, then teachers on this path. The filaments spread, wove together, and spread again into the dreaming of this book.

[5] Bridging is incorporated into all of my teaching. See http://megbeeler.com

[6] Pearl, Eric. *The Reconnection: Heal Others, Heal Yourself.* New York: Hay House, Inc., 2001.

[7] Attributed to many native North American tribes, including Apache, Cherokee, and Lenape. One version, as told to Tèmakamoxkomëhèt by his friend Asuwibi'oxkw of the Lenape tribe, quoted on http://www.nativeamericanembassy.net/ www.lenni-lenape.com/www/html/LenapeArchives/LenapeSet-01/feedwich.html.

CHAPTER 2

[1] Salzberg, Sharon. "Meditation: The Key to Resilience in Caregiving," 17 Nov. 2011, *Huffington Post.* http://www.huffingtonpost.com/sharon-salzberg/ meditation-caregiving-resilience_b_784122.html.

[2] Eighty percent of the fat cells you burn during exercise are expelled through your breath. Bloom, Barbara, oral teaching, December 2014. See www.bloominsideout.com.

[3] Desai, Panache, "Discover Your Soul Signature" interview with Christine Kloser for *Transformational Author Experience*, May, 2014.

[4] Andrews, Dr. Synthia. *The Path of Energy: Awaken Your Personal Power and Expand Your Consciousness.* Pompton Plains, N.J.: The Career Press, Inc., 2011, p. 78.

[5] Wangyal, Tenzin. *Healing with Form, Energy, and Light: The Five Elements in Tibetan Shamanism, Tantra, and Dzogchen.* (Ithaca, New York: Snow Lion Publications, 2002), p. xviii.

[6] Tolle, Eckhart. *A New Earth: Awakening to Your Life's Purpose.* (New York: Penguin Group, 2006), p. 144.

[7] Baraz, James and Shoshana Alexander. *Awakening Joy: 10 Steps That Will Put You on the Road to Real Happiness.* (Berkeley: Parallax Press, 2012), p. xviii.

CHAPTER 3

[1] Zavala, Eda. Personal conversation, Santa Rosa CA, Sept. 9, 2007

[2] Quispé, Humberto Sonqo. Lecture at Mt. Shasta, California, September, 2011.

[3] Quispé, loc.cit.

[4] The practice of releasing heavy energy without rejecting it or clinging to it aligns with both Jungian and Buddhist practices of relating to the shadow rather than cutting it off. In Buddhism, it is called mindfulness: focusing one's awareness on the present moment while calmly acknowledging and accepting one's feelings, thoughts, and bodily sensations.

[5] Hanh, Thich Nhat. *The Last Tree*, in Dharma Gaia, ed. Allan Hunt Badiner. (Berkeley, CA.: Parallax Press, 1990), 220.

CHAPTER 4

[1] Prider, Angela. http://www.westcoastshamanic.com/Apprenticeship/white-bone-shamanic-arts-apprenticeship.

[2] The seven chakras in yogic practice, different in location but somewhat similar in use to d'an tien, are energetic vortices that take in and release energy or life force.

[3] In Inca/Q'ero cosmology, there are diverse types of living energies. The three centers/three planes of existence are distinguished by the qualities of energy you find there. *Llank'ay*, representing the first three chakras and the *qosqo*, is the power of sacred action and service. It is physical energy that corresponds with *uhu pacha*, the interior world of lower, subconscious energy. *Munay* represents unconditional love, respect, and appreciation for everything. It corresponds with the 4th chakra and with *kaypacha*, the everyday, middle world of material energy. *Yachay*, representing chakras 6, 7, and 8, is wisdom, and impersonal power grounded in intellect. It corresponds with *hanaq' pacha*, the upper world of light and energy.

[4] Yábar, Américo. Oral teaching, November 1996.

[5] Rohr, Richard. *Mysticism: Three Ways to See the Sunset.* September 2012. http://thevalueofsparrows.com/2012/09/13/mysticism-three-ways-to-see-the-sunset-by-richard-rohr/.

[6] Apffel-Marglin, Frederique, ed., and PRATEC (the Andean Project for Peasant Technology). *The Spirit of Regeneration: Andean Culture Confronting Western Notions of Development.* London: Zed Books, 1998.

CHAPTER 5

[1] Krippner, Stanley. Society for the Study of Shamanism Conference. September 2014. Panel discussion.

[2] Soul loss is often a result of trauma; soul retrieval and remembering, an ancient shamanic practice, can help you reconnect with your essence and the wholeness you were born with. See, for example, Tick, Edward. *War and the Soul: Healing Our Nation's Veterans from Post-Traumatic Stress Disorder.* Wheaton, Illinois: Quest Books, 2005, and Ingerman, Sandra. *Soul Retrieval: Mending the Fragmented Self.* NY: HarperSanFrancisco, 2006.

[3] Larson, Cynthia Sue. *Shift the World With Deep Listening.* January 2013. http://cynthiasuelarson.wordpress.com.

CHAPTER 6

[1] Wangyal, *Healing,* xviii.

[2] I learned this form of the elements meditation from Elizabeth Jenkins.

[3] Young, Jon. Oral teaching, Petaluma, CA. June 30, 2012. See Thomas, Elizabeth Marshall. *The Old Way: A Story of the First People.* (New York: Farrarr Strauss Giroux, 2006), 269. The author recounts being told that "star sickness"—the dissent, anger, and jealousy that drive people apart and damage the unity central to life on the savannah—is removed in these trance dances.

[4] Yoga teachers advise against using the fire breath if you are pregnant or on your moon cycle.

[5] Keeney, Bradford. *Adapted from Shaking Medicine: The Healing Power of Ecstatic Movement, in Spirituality & Health,* May-June 2007, http://spiritualityhealth.com/articles/shaking-medicine.

[6] Yábar, Américo. Personal teaching in Peru, 1996.

[7] This practice is described in Villoldo, Alberto. *Shaman, Healer, Sage: How to Heal Yourself and Others with the Energy Medicine of the Americas.* (New York: Harmony Books, 2000), 54–55.

[8] Hafiz, Shams-ud-din Muhammad. *Awake Awhile,* in Daniel Ladinsky, ed., *I Heard God Laughing: Renderings of Hafiz.* (Oakland, CA: Mobius Press, 1999), 73.

[9] Whyte, David. Crossing the Unknown Sea: Work as a Pilgrimage of Identity. New York: Riverhead Books, 2002, retrieved from http://www.gratefulness.org/readings/whyte_dsr.htm.

[10] Chodron, Pema, *The Places That Scare You: A Guide to Fearlessness in Difficult Times.* Boston: Shambhala Publications, 2007.

[11] Yábar, Américo. Personal conversation, 1998.

CHAPTER 7

[1] Villoldo, Alberto. *Courageous Dreaming: How Shamans Dream the World Into Being.* Carlsbad, CA: Hay House, Inc., 2008. Originally found on www.thefourwinds.com.

[2] There are many varieties of the healing ball taught by qi gong teachers. See one version on YouTube at http://www.youtube.com/watch?v=TsAmbkINMgo&feature=related.

[3] Spangler, David. "David's Desk: #59 Grail Space", April 2012. *Lorian Association.* http://lorianassociation.com/59-grail-space.

[4] Spangler, loc.cit.

[5] The spiritual "sun behind the sun" has meaning in both indigenous and Gnostic cosmology. It is connected with the Fifth World we are moving into, according to Hopi cosmology. For me it holds the energy of potential, of Dreaming, and of what we are creating.

[6] Nearly all Bushmen have been forcibly relocated by surrounding governments since the 1970s, away from their traditional hunter-gatherer lands and into settlements. The Naro San Bushmen inhabit the central Kalahari desert in Botswana. While "San" is the official and academically accepted name, and the one used by tracker Jon Young, most Bushmen call themselves Bushmen, not San. According to Elizabeth Marshall Thomas, "san" was a derogatory term used originally by the Khoikhoi people.

[7] Young, Jon. *What the Robin Knows: How Birds Reveal Secrets of the Natural World.* (New York: Houghton Mifflin Harcourt, 2012), xvi.

CHAPTER 8

[1] Shamanic journeying is a powerful way to explore the unseen worlds in cooperation with spirit helpers. This ancient, worldwide, experiential practice of engaging with the forces of the natural world takes you into visionary states and altered experience of "reality" without the assistance of ingested substances.

[2] Since dark matter cannot be seen directly, these filaments are difficult to observe. But using the Hubble Space Telescope in 2012, astronomers have created images in 3D. See http://www.space.com/18071-dark-matter-fossil-of-the-big-bang-found-video.html.

[3] *Ceke*, the Quechua word for cord, also refers to a filament that connects you to everything with *kawsay*, or life force: the cosmos, sun, stars, mountains, sacred lakes, trees, stones, rivers, clouds, animals, and humans. Where ley lines are magnetic field connections that can be felt within the earth, ceke lines are human-and-earth created.

[4] Forms of this meditation exist in many cultures, and I have deep gratitude to all those who led me to this awareness: the Q'ero/Inca people of the Andes, Américo Yábar, and Martin Gray. The meditation has evolved and blossomed into the present

form in my spiritual practice over the course of twenty years, feeding and weaving all of us who use it into the great web.

[5] Silko, Leslie Marmon. *The Turquoise Ledge*. (NY: Viking, 2010), 130, 136, 141.

[6] Emoto, Masaru. End-of-the-year message, December 2004 email.

CHAPTER 9

[1] Eisenstein, Charles. *The More Beautiful World Our Hearts Know Is Possible*. Berkeley: North Atlantic Books, 2013.

[2] www.shinrin-yoku.org.

[3] Storeide, Morten Wolf. The World Drum Project.

[4] The Nature Speaks project, with in-depth interviews of twenty-two people who communicate with trees, offers further insight. http://www.naturespeaks.org/.

[5] Hanh, *Tree*, 218—219.

[6] Hanh, loc. cit.

[7] Bernie Krause coined the term biophony and helped define the structure of sound-scape ecology. He has recorded and archived pristine sound environments from around the world. See *The Great Animal Orchestra: Finding the Origins of Music in the World's Wild Places*, New York: Little, Brown, 2012. Entrainment in a biomusi-cological sense occurs when your organism synchronizes with an external rhythm.

[8] "Tree Hugging Now Scientifically Validated," *Uplift*, Dec. 2012, http://50.28.60.91/~upliftme/index.php/people/natural-healing/521-tree-hugging-scientifically-val-idated.

[9] Miller, Henry. Quoted in Alberto Villoldo, *Courageous Dreaming*. (New York: Hay House, 2008), 77.

CHAPTER 10

[1] Krause, *Orchestra*, 27 & 31.

[2] Emoto, Masaru. *The Hidden Messages in Water*. New York: Atria, 2005.

[3] Raygorodetsky, Gieb. "Restoring the Sacred Web of Life in Siberia's Golden Moun-tains," *National Geographic*, April 7, 2011. http://newswatch.nationalgeographic.com/2011/04/07/altai_golden-mountains_russia-pictures/.

[4] Charing, Howard G. "Communion With The Infinite – The Visual Music of the Ship-ibo Tribe of the Amazon," http://www.ayahuasca.com/spirit/primordial-and-tra-ditional-culture/communion-with-the-infinite-the-visual-music-of-the-shipibo-tribe-of-the-amazon/. Thanks also to Richard Down for personal communications on Shipibo weave and song.

[5] Charing, loc. cit.

[6] A mantra is a sound, syllable, word, or group of words considered to be capable of creating transformation. Mantras originated in the Vedic tradition of India, becoming a customary practice within Hinduism, Buddhism, Sikhism, and Jainism and some contemporary meditation practices. Retrieved from http://en.wikipedia.org/wiki/Mantra.

[7] The six syllables in om mani padme hum are said to represent the purification of the six realms of existence. The Dalai Lama writes "... in dependence on the practice of a path which is an indivisible union of method and wisdom, you can transform your impure body, speech, and mind into the pure exalted body, speech, and mind of a Buddha ... These frequencies ... act as a harmonic sound resonance against blocking energy, or sleeping energy. Plants reflect this action as well because of the phonetic strength of vibration that is stimulated by natural pronunciation." H. H. Tenzin Gyatso, 14th Dalai Lama. "Om Mani Padme Hum." http://en.wikipedia.org/wiki/Aum_Mani_Padme_Hum.

[8] Many sound healing modalities are based on energy shifting. One of the oldest, the Tomatis sound sensory integration stimulation, focuses on mitigating learning, language, and emotional difficulties; www.tomatis.com. Jonathan Goldman is another good source of information; www.healingsounds.com/.

[9] Carr, Nicholas. The Shallows: What the Internet Is Doing to Our Brains. (NY: Norton, 2010), 219.

[10] Yábar, Américo. Personal conversation, 1998.

[11] Dispenza, "Evolve Brain."

[12] Bryan, Leslie. "Full Moon Meditation," in "Healing Journey: Comfort, Care, Compassion," August 2012 email.

[13] Olson, Danielle Prohom. http://bodydivineyoga.wordpress.com/.

CHAPTER 11

[1] Gandhi, Mahatma, http://www.quotesworthrepeating.com/quote-by/m/mohandas-gandhi/notable-quotation-spoken-of-mohandas-gandhi/. Variants are attributed to many other authors.

[2] Schlitz, Marilyn, Cassandra Vieten, and Tina Amorok. The Art and Science of Transformation in Everyday Life. Oakland: New Harbinger Publications, 2008.

[3] Carr, Shallows, 184.

[4] Spangler, "Grail Space."

[5] Scull, Sandy. "Against the Talons of Winter Blues." Personal correspondence.

[6] Chopra, Deepak. Quoted in Ratigan, Dylan, "Save Yourself to Save the World." 29 July 2011. *Business Insider.* http://www.businessinsider.com/save-yourself-to-save-the-world-2011-7.

CHAPTER 12

[1] Dyer, Wayne. *The Power of Intention: Learning to Co-create Your World Your Way.* New York: Hay House, 2011.

[2] Despite a recurrence of cancer, Joan continues with her intent to be present and fluid with all that comes her way.

[3] Chopra, Deepak. 'I Will Not Be Pleased' -- Your Health and the Nocebo Effect." 26 September 2012. *Huffington Post.* http://www.huffingtonpost.com/deepak-chopra/nocebo-effect_b_1811290.html.

[4] Love talking, or Geancannach, comes from the Celtic tradition by way of Tom Cowan. See http://www.riverdrum.com/.

[5] Wolkstein, Diane and Samuel N. Kramer. *Inanna: Queen of Heaven and Earth.* NY: Harper and Row, 1983.

[6] Sandra Ingerman initiated this practice of weaving a web of light at the full moon in 2000.

[7] Coined by Vietnamese Zen master Thich Nhat Hanh to describe the Buddha's core teaching of dependent co-arising, as well as the relationship of open systems characterized by some theorists as "interexistence."

CHAPTER 13

[1] Fox, Matthew and Rupert Sheldrake. *The Physics of Angels: Exploring the Realm Where Science and Spirit Meet.* (NY: Harper Collins, 1996), 141–42.

[2] Millay, Jean. International Conference on Shamanism, Healing, and Transformation. Panel discussion. San Rafael, CA, 2014.

[3] Quesada, Oscar Miro. Interview with Christina Pratt. *Why Shamanism Now.* October 2012, http://whyshamanismnow.com/2012/10/the-vital-evolutionary-role-of-shamanism-with-don-oscar-miro-quesada/.

[4] In this meditation—before we traveled to the jungle—I was dismembered. I saw myself become compost, and out of the compost saw a seed (the new me) growing. The meditation foretold deep and transformative change that informed and helped me understand the rest of my journey.

[5] Miller, Elizabeth. Personal correspondence. August 2012.

[6] Feighery-Ross, Moria. Personal correspondence. August 2012. The trees aligning with meditators study she refers to is Bernie Kraus's (see chapter 10).

[7] Lewis, Thomas MD, Fari Amini, MD, and Richard Lannon, MD. *A General Theory of Love.* NY: Vintage (reprint) 2001.

[8] Spangler, "Grail Space."

[9] Thomas, *Old Way,* 267.

[10] Edward Lorenz coined this term. Small differences in initial conditions yield widely divergent outcomes for chaotic systems, from weather to human interactions. Each choice we make in our lives has an infinite possibility of effects on others. http://en.wikipedia.org/wiki/Butterfly_effect.

[11] Gorgo, Lauren C. "The Phases of Embodiment." 2011. http://spiritlibrary.com/lauren-c-gorgo/the-phases-of-embodiment.

[12] Sheldrake's theory of morphic resonance is vehemently debated within the scientific community, providing another example of how belief affects perception. http://en.wikipedia.org/wiki/Rupert_Sheldrake.

[13] See, for example, Peterson, Brenda. *Living By Water: Essays on Life, Land, and Spirit.* Alaska Northwest Books,1991. Also see Frohuff and Peterson, eds., *Between Species: Celebrating the Dolphin-Human Bond,* Sierra Club Books, 2003.

[14] Lindsay, Muriel. *The Dolphin Letters: Vital Information from Sea to Land.* (Cardiff-by-the Sea: Waterfront Press, 2013), Letter 7.

CHAPTER 14

[1] Hanh, Thich Nat. http://www.guardian.co.uk/sustainable-business/zen-thich-naht-hanh-buddhidm-business-values.

[2] Delgado, Jorge Luis. *Andean Awakening.* Quoted in http://www.incaglossary.org/a.html.

[3] Quispé, Humberto Sonqo. Oral teaching, San Jose State University, California, November, 2008.

[4] Thomas, *Old Way,* 221–23.

[5] Turk, *Raven's Gift,* 87–88.

[6] Jenkins, Elizabeth B. *Initiation: A Woman's Spiritual Adventure in the Heart of the Andes.* (New York; G. P. Putnam's Sons, 1997), 244.

[7] Jenkins, loc.cit.

[8] Much has changed since the 1990s when I first visited. Western clothing and speaking Spanish are far more widespread.

[9] See Meyerson, Julia. *Tambo: Life in an Andean Village.* Austin: University of Texas Press, 1990. Also, see Webb, Hillary S. *Yanantin and Masintin in the Andean World: Complementary Dualism in Modern Peru.* (Albuquerque: University of New Mexico Press, 2012), 40–41.

[10] In their home communities, these healers serve whomever comes, sometimes seeing up to fifty people a day (in Nepal), and receive whatever offerings their clients can afford, rather than charging set fees.

[11] Xqamxebe, Nqate. Quoted in 1998 film *The Great Dance: A Hunter's Story.*

[12] See Hill, Julia. *The Legacy of Luna: The Story of a Tree, a Woman and the Struggle to Save the Redwoods.* New York: HarperOne, 2001.

[13] Wilcox, Joan Parisi. *Keepers of the Ancient Knowledge: The Mystical World of the Q'ero Indians of Peru.* (Boston: Element Books, Inc., 1999), 10.

[14] Crowfoot, Blackfoot warrior and orator, 1821–90. http://www.shannonthunderbird.com/Elders%20Speak.htm.

[15] Projects such as the Global Coherence Initiative and global random number generators, measuring effects of world events, show unexpected structure apparently associated with major world events. See http://www.heartmath.org/gci/ and http://noetic.org.

[16] Seed, John, Joanna Macy, Pat Fleming, and Arne Naess. *Thinking Like a Mountain: Towards a Council of All Beings.* (Philadelphia: New Society Publishers, 1988), 79–90 (narrative) and 97–113 (full description). For online instructions and alternative forms, see Elizabeth Bragg and Ruth Rosenhek. *The Council of All Beings Workshop Manual* 1998–2001, at http://www.rainforestinfo.org.au/deep-eco/cabcont.htm.

[17] Benedetti, Fabrizio. Quoted in Cara Feinberg, "The Placebo Phenomenon," *Harvard Magazine,* January-February 2013. http://harvardmagazine.com/2013/01/the-placebo-phenomenon.

[18] Gonzales, OmeAkaEhekatl Erick. "The Importance of Councils." *Earth Peoples United.* 17 July 2009. http://www.earthpeoplesunited.org/gatherings.

[19] Nunez del Prado, Juan and Ivan Nunez del Prado. Oral teaching, Oregon, May 2010.

[20] Retrieved from http://noetic.org/directory/person/edgar-mitchell/.

[21] Berry, Wendell. "Manifesto: The Mad Farmer Liberation Front" (excerpt), in *Collected Poems.* Retrieved from https://www.goodreads.com/author/quotes/8567.Wendell_Berry.

[22] For some shamanic resources and my personal bibliography of shamanic literature, see http://megbeeler.com.

[23] Immersions are a traditional aspect of African water ways. For more information on Mandaza, see Ortiz-Hill, Michael and Mandaza Augustine Kandemwa. *Twin From Another Tribe: The Story of Two Shamanic Healers from Africa and North America.* Wheaton, IL: Quest Books, 2007.

CHAPTER 15

[1] Transfiguration is an ancient practice found in many spiritual traditions. See Ingerman, Sandra. *Medicine for the Earth: How To Transform Personal and Environmental Toxins.* (New York: Three Rivers Press, 2000), 189–98.

[2] Ingerman, Sandra, oral transmission.

[3] Talbot, Michael. *The Holographic Universe.* (London: HarperCollins Publishers, 1991), 104–5.

[4] Talbot, *Holographic,* 6.

[5] Braden, Gregg. *The Spontaneous Healing of Belief: Shattering the Paradigm of False Limits.* (New York: Hay House, 2008), v.

[6] Talbot, *Holographic,* 93.

[7] Wolynn, Mark. The Hellinger Institute of Northern California. http://hellingerpa.com/cases.shtml.

[8] Myss, Carolyn. *Anatomy of The Spirit: The Seven Stages of Healing.* New York: Three Rivers Press, 1996.

[9] Rumi, Jelalludin, quoted by Coleman Barks in an interview: http://www.sfgate.com/living/article/Coleman-Barks-foremost-Rumi-translator-talks-2537796.php#page-2.

[10] Roy, Arundhati. "Come September," in *War Talk.* (Cambridge: South End Press, 2003), 75.

[11] Larson, Cynthia Sue. *Reality Shifts: When Consciousness Changes the Physical World.* (Berkeley: Reality Shifters, 1999), Chapter 8.

[12] For more on deep listening, see http:// mindful.org/deep-listening.

[13] Patanjali. *Yoga Sutras* 1.12–1.16, as summarized at http://www.swamij.com/yoga-sutras-11216.htm.

[14] Dalai Lama. *The Dalai Lama at Harvard.* (Snow Lion USA, 1988), 37.

[15] Shamanism is the oldest spiritual practice across the globe, dating back thirty to fifty thousand years. The non-attachment aspect of shamanism is referred to as "becoming a hollow bone," a vehicle for spirit, without any personal ego attachment.

[16] Pradervand, Pierre. *The Gentle Art of Blessing: A Simple Practice That Will Transform You and Your World.* (New York: Atria Paperback/Beyond Words Publishing, Inc. 2009), 2.

[17] Sparenberg, David. *Life in the Age of Extinctions.* (Helsinki: Ovi Project Publications, 2012), 19.

ACKNOWLEDGEMENTS

I am profoundly grateful for my connection with the living universe, earth who sustains us, stars who light our way, and the mystery behind it all.

The roots of this book run deep. My uncle John McSweeny showed me the power of touching soil to learn about it. My mother Margaret Olsen encouraged my curiosity. My aunt Patricia McSweeny loved me unconditionally and believed I could accomplish whatever I set out to do.

The mountains, stones, and lagoons in the Andes opened the world of living energy to me. The Q'ero nation and other Quechua-speaking people in the Andes modeled joyful alignment and reciprocity; they showed me the power and possibility of union with the heart of the universe.

Américo Yábar taught me to flow in the rivers of energy between heart, earth, and cosmos. S. N. Goenka helped me experience the power of silence and observation through Vipassana. Wonderful teachers from around the world—Sandra Ingerman, Tito La Rosa, Joanna Macy, Mandaza Augustine Kandemwa, Tom Cowan, Helen McCarthy, Reclaiming, Four Winds, the Foundation for Shamanic Studies, and others—helped me expand my relationship with spirit and the worlds outside space and time. Phil Madden introduced me to the world of qi and kept me laughing. My power animals and spirit helpers guide me daily in visioning a future of reciprocity, sustainability and harmony for us all.

I thank my friend and mentor Ginny Anderson for walking this path with me for over 30 years. My fellow explorers of earth, energy, and cosmos—Claudia Comerci, Carol Crestetto, Ellen Henson, Moria Feighery-Ross, Heidi Irgens, Elizabeth Miller, Cathlene Richmond, Ann Riley, Linea Stewart, and Valerie Wolf—make my heart sing with the depth, bliss, and joy we share. My journey circle—Christina Bertea, Jeff Brown, Christine Donohue, Cameron McKinley, Linda Milks, Claude Poncelet, Noelle Poncelet, Sandy Skull, Pat Usner, and Julia Weaver— support my wild curiosity and invoke the spirits to help and guide me whenever I ask.

My hundreds of students and clients have welcomed my wisdom and experience with openness and enthusiasm; I thank you all for teaching me with every interaction.

Those who reviewed early versions of the manuscript—Ginny Anderson, Claudia Comerci, Moria Feighery-Ross, Ann Riley, Joanna Harcourt Smith, José Luis Gómez Soler, Susan Thompson, Kate Vasha—and my editor Sheridan McCarthy gave me support, courage, and good feedback just when I needed them.

I am grateful to my daughter Maria Fernanda Olsen-Beeler von Tersch for opening my heart daily. To my husband and partner of 32 years, Tom von Tersch, who is my sounding board, hand holder, and love, thank you for sharing the path of life and the river of Being with me.

This book has been a collaboration guided with love, intent, and spirit. I thank all of you.

INDEX

About the Author

Meg Beeler, M.A. is an internationally known author, shamanic healer, and Energy Alchemy expert. She translates ancient wisdom into simple practices for connecting with the power of nature and the universe.

A passionate explorer of wholeness and consciousness, Meg has traveled extensively, from the high mountains of the Andes and Himalayas to the savannahs of Africa and the jungles of the Amazon. She is a graduate of U. C. Berkeley and Antioch College.

Her lifelong inquiry into healing the heart and lifting the spirit drew her into the indigenous teachings that would transform her life. Meg's adopted daughter and her husband taught her the power of connection. Working at Apple, and later authoring over 20 award-winning technical books, taught her to write clear instructions. Meg grounds herself with organic gardening, walking the land, and perceiving the interrelationships that sustain life.

Integrating her experience with shamanism, meditation, Andean energy healing, and Qigong galvanized Meg to create Energy Alchemy, her system for changing suffering and blockages into joy through reconnection with nature. She guides and inspires workshop participants and clients with practical spiritual tools and transcendent learning experiences in workshops worldwide.

Meg is the founder of Earth Caretakers, dedicated to bringing to life our collective dream of a more beautiful world. She lives in the San Francisco Bay Area. www.megbeeler.com

32822881R00147

Made in the USA
Middletown, DE
20 June 2016